D0593885

"In a world that continues to demand more, Neen's honest insights, powerful research and bubbly humor drives home the importance of managing internal and external factors to reclaim our time and attention. I recommend this book to everyone, at every level, looking for winning attention strategies to lead a more fulfilled, productive and intentional life."

—Mary Rooney,
Vice President, Strategic Planning
and Communications, Comcast Spotlight

"In the business world where leaders are often distracted and overwhelmed, this book provides solutions every person can implement in their personal and professional life.

Leading a life of significance requires you to pay attention to who, and what really matters. Neen's attention frameworks and strategies make this a must-read for anyone wanting to be a more current, relevant and influential leader.

I am recommending the staff and students at High Point University follow Ms. James advice to be more thoughtful each day, more productive each week, and more responsible each year."

—Dr. Nido R. Qubein,
President, High Point University

"There's no one who knows—or pays—attention like Neen James. That means there's no one better to help you understand not only why attention is so important in our 'Attention Deficit Society,' but also to guide you through shifting into the kind of intentional attention that really pays. Full of insight, research, and straight talk—just like Neen herself!—this book should be required reading for anyone who wants to truly gain control of their work and life."

—Tamsen Webster, Co-Producer TEDx Cambridge, Founder of Red Thread

"Attention Pays is a masterclass in how to influence others, win business and lead teams. In a world where everybody is crazy busy, this book gives you the tools to cut through the clutter so you're seen, heard, and understood. I've made it required reading for my staff and clients."

—Michael Port, NY Times, WSJ Bestselling author of *Steal the Show*

"Attention Pays captures the most important thing everyone wants in this world, other's attention. Everyone wants to feel important and Neen James shares how to do just that in this wonderful book that every leader & team member should read. Welcome to the Attention Revolution!"

—John R. DiJulius III, Author of *The Customer Service Revolution*

"What I appreciate so much about Neen's very attentive (to the reader!) book is this: being attentive isn't just a binary goal (e.g., you are either paying attention or you aren't). It's a practice. Focusing on Intentional Attention lets us forgive ourselves for those lapses we all have—but gives us a tool box to put successful attention "in our way"—which in turn puts success in our way. Turn off your phone, and read this book."

—Tom Webster,
Vice President, Strategy, Edison Research

"After an extremely successful and provocative read with Folding Time, Neen James hits another home run with Attention Pays. There were so many powerful messages around being highly productive, but through an ever changing personal and professional landscape – we have lost the ability to give our undivided attention. This consistently happens in the workplace and unfortunately, outside of the workplace as well. We have to be intentionally investing all the time, there's no other choice. The rewards are immeasurable."

—Bob O'Brien,
Vice President, Southwest Region,
Comcast Spotlight

"There are teachers and gurus, innovators and thought
leaders. And then there is Neen James. Years ago
when we met, I was immediately struck by her power
to ignite a room, to change how people think about
themselves, and to demonstrate what is possible if we
pay attention and create a life of intention. Neen's
power is in her authenticity. She absolutely talks the talk
(like no other), but Neen truly walks the walk—and,
in those signature pink heels, no less.

Neen values relationship and service to others above all
else. She is a passionate connector of people, and one
of the most generous professionals I've ever met.
Neen changed my life for the better, and when you
immerse yourself in Attention Pays, she will
no doubt change yours."

—Elizabeth Lucas-Averett (Ella),
Host of On Air with Ella

"Neen James has written a brilliant book that demands
us all to sit up and pay attention. From the insightful
research on the costs of inattention to the practical tips
and strategies that allow us to harness the power of
intentional attention in all walks of our lives, this book is a
must read for anyone who wants to be more focused,
more productive and have more impact on the world."

—Toni Newman,
Founder of The Innovation Advantage,
Professional Catalyst

"Stop everything you are doing and join the Attention Revolution, led by the inimitable Neen James. In this chaotic and cacophonic world, Neen teaches you to control what demands your attention, and to prioritize what really matters, with equal parts love, humor, and brilliance. This book is essential reading for every leader who cares about their relationships at home, at work, and in their community."

—Laura Gassner Otting, Chief Confidence Catalyst

"In Attention Pays Neen brings the business world closer to building real relationships. We are in a time-stressed world, responding to demands of others and jump at every phone's notification, taking us away from people in front of us. This has a negative impact on relationships and success. In a frenzied environment, and we miss chances to connect. Neen's attention strategies help us focus on everyday important interactions, help control distractions, improve connections and live each precious moments. This focus helps me be a better employee, father, and husband. This book helps your organization analyze factors diminishing your attention and put the care back in your relationships with customers, clients, and employees. You will find that attention pays."

—Scott D. Ferrin, Field Director, Society for Human Resource Management (SHRM)

"Attention Pays reads like a business book for the inefficient and exhausted. But it's actually a field guide to living your life with more balance, intention, focus, joy. Sneaky move, Neen."

—Ann Handley, WSJ Bestselling Author of *Everybody Writes* & Chief Content Officer, MarketingProfs

"From the moment Neen shared this idea with me, I knew she had a winner. Her unique perspective on this important topic is critical for all leaders today. Attention Pays will help businesses stay relevant, leaders improve morale, and individuals grow business relationships or the bottom line. I recommend this book to anyone who wants to differentiate themselves...from leaders who want to stand out, to parents who want to create more significant memories with their kids, the message is clear: Attention Pays."

—Clint Greenleaf, CEO, HomePlate Peanut Butter

"Do yourself a big life-changing favor and take the wise lessons of Attention Pays to heart and you will morph in really important ways. Neen James helps you tame the "squirrels" of the un-focused brain to lead you to a personal and professional life of effectiveness, well-being and enormous impact."

—Scott Halford, Wall Street Journal Bestselling Author of *Activate Your Brain*, Member National Speakers Hall of Fame

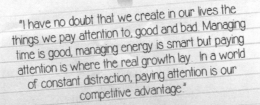

"I have no doubt that we create in our lives the things we pay attention to, good and bad. Managing time is good, managing energy is smart but paying attention is where the real growth lay. In a world of constant distraction, paying attention is our competitive advantage."

—Matt Church, Founder of Thought Leaders Global

"A devastating indictment of flawed time management and bogus multitasking, Attention Pays will rewire how you do EVERYTHING. Your to-do list should have exactly one item: buy this book."

—Jay Baer,
Founder of Convince & Convert and
Author of *Hug Your Haters*

"If you wish you could focus on what matters, stop doing things that rob you of profit and success, and improve interaction with business colleagues, clients and loved ones, then slap your distracted self and pick up Attention Pays by Neen James. It'll change your life."

—Ian Altman,
Bestselling Co-Author of *Same Side Selling*

"You and I have been admonished by parents and others to "Pay attention!" Less likely have you been told that attention pays as Neen James does in this insightful and practical new book. If you want to be a more effective leader or just live a fuller, richer life, then I recommend you read this book."

—Mark Sanborn,
Speaker and Author of *The Fred Factor*
and *The Potential Principle*

"It turns out we can't manage our time, we can only manage our attention. In this insightful book, Neen James shows us how being more intentional with our attention helps us get the results we want at work, at home and in our communities.

Put down your phone and read this book. It will forever change how you pay attention.

Learning how to pay intentional attention personally, professionally and globally can change every aspect of your life. In Attention Pays, Neen James gives you the playbook."

—Clay Hebert,
Founder of Clarity and Growth

"I had no idea the cost of inattention. Neen James gave me an insight into this topic that I really needed to hear! Neen is so spot-on with her insight into what is ailing us. Not only costing us in our pockets but in our health. This is an important read. Don't read this book unless you are serious about getting your act together! I put it down in the middle and actually did what Neen suggests and it helped my focus immediately."

—Laurie Guest CSP, Guest Enterprises, Inc.

ATTENTION PAYS

ATTENTION PAYS

HOW TO DRIVE PROFITABILITY, PRODUCTIVITY, AND ACCOUNTABILITY

NEEN JAMES

Copyright ©2018 by John Wiley & Sons, Inc. All rights reserved.

Published by John Wiley & Sons, Inc., Hoboken, New Jersey.
Published simultaneously in Canada.

Attention Pays is a trademark of Neen James.

No part of this publication may be reproduced, stored in a retrieval system, or transmitted in any form or by any means, electronic, mechanical, photocopying, recording, scanning, or otherwise, except as permitted under Section 107 or 108 of the 1976 United States Copyright Act, without either the prior written permission of the Publisher, or authorization through payment of the appropriate per-copy fee to the Copyright Clearance Center, Inc., 222 Rosewood Drive, Danvers, MA 01923, (978) 750-8400, fax (978) 646-8600, or on the Web at www.copyright .com. Requests to the Publisher for permission should be addressed to the Permissions Department, John Wiley & Sons, Inc., 111 River Street, Hoboken, NJ 07030, (201) 748-6011, fax (201) 748-6008, or online at http://www.wiley.com/go/permissions.

Limit of Liability/Disclaimer of Warranty: While the publisher and author have used their best efforts in preparing this book, they make no representations or warranties with respect to the accuracy or completeness of the contents of this book and specifically disclaim any implied warranties of merchantability or fitness for a particular purpose. No warranty may be created or extended by sales representatives or written sales materials. The advice and strategies contained herein may not be suitable for your situation. You should consult with a professional where appropriate. Neither the publisher nor author shall be liable for any loss of profit or any other commercial damages, including but not limited to special, incidental, consequential, or other damages.

For general information on our other products and services or for technical support, please contact our Customer Care Department within the United States at (800) 762-2974, outside the United States at (317) 572-3993 or fax (317) 572-4002.

Wiley publishes in a variety of print and electronic formats and by print-on-demand. Some material included with standard print versions of this book may not be included in e-books or in print-on-demand. If this book refers to media such as a CD or DVD that is not included in the version you purchased, you may download this material at http://booksupport.wiley.com. For more information about Wiley products, visit www.wiley.com.

Library of Congress Cataloging-in-Publication Data is Available:

ISBN 9781119480259 (Hardcover)
ISBN 9781119481355 (ePDF)
ISBN 9781119480525 (ePub)

Cover Design: Wiley

Printed in the United States of America

10 9 8 7 6 5 4 3 2 1

To you, my brilliant friend.

Your beautiful mind showed me
the power of attention.

To you, my brilliant reader.
Your undivided attention is the greatest gift
you can give someone.

Today, invest one minute, in one interaction,
to create one significant moment,
for just one person that may create
one memory that will last a lifetime.

—Neen James

Contents

CONTENTS

CONTENTS

Contents

Contents

List of Illustrations

A Love Note From Neen

G'Day, (that's Aussie for hello)

You're pretty cool for reading a dedication and not skipping ahead, thanks for doing that.

The book you're holding is the result of hours of conversations, hundreds of presentations to amazing audiences, and much laughter (admittedly a few tears), and now I am setting it free in the world. That's a little scary. The reason for writing this book is to get the world to truly pay attention to each other, and not everyone gets that. But you do. Maybe that's why you picked up this book?

I want you to look up at the magnificent world around you and really notice people. I want you to take a moment and look someone deeply in the eyes. I want you to pause, take a breath, and be right here in this very moment.

I want everyone to feel seen and heard. I don't want anyone to ever feel invisible.

You're my favorite for investing in this book. Yes, you. Thank you for investing your precious attention in reading and sharing it with others.

You are the most important person right now.

My deepest appreciation extends to my incredible clients and audiences that have invited me to stand in service of them and share perspectives and stories. Thank you all for sharing inspiring notes, posts on social media and comments on how you have applied these attention strategies in your lives—my life is richer because of you.

My deep love and admiration goes to the people listed here who have inspired, challenged, and supported me in this process. Yes, it's risky to share a list knowing I might forget someone. I adore these people.

- My Andy ~ balancing my crazy 'all-in' with your calm. You are my world.

- Meg ~ You are my person. Everyone needs someone as loyal, authentic, smart, funny and caring as you. You know everything.

- My family ~ in both countries, for constant encouragement.

- Maria ~ can't do life without you.

- Misty ~ your friendship and prayers. I am forever grateful.

- Candy ~ may there be more soufflé moments, cocktails and kaftans.

- Eileen ~ walk and talks are the best therapy, you keep me grounded.

- Donovan ~ I will forever listen with my eyes because of you.

- Patrick, Judson, Stacey, Jon ~ you help me think differently, giggle loudly and celebrate everything.

- Tami ~ You are remarkable and you are a gift to me.

- Michael ~ thinking and performing bigger, because of you—thank you for being my advocate.

- Scott ~ your friendship and community continue to elevate everything. Speak and Spill is my business family.

- Mark ~ you changed the direction of my business and challenge me daily.

- Simon ~ you inspired me to create an attention movement.

- Tamsen ~ helping find my red thread and inspiring me to be smarter—you are a great accountability partner.

- JJ ~ your constant encouragement and reminder 'It's You against You' thank you for being my cheerleader.

- Theo ~ Your gifts of compassion, generosity, and discernment make the world a better place. Amazing.

- Clay ~ your clarity is a gift to the world, your friendship and your brain are a gift to me. This book is better because of you and all our virtual writing dates.

- Phil ~ listening, encouraging and being on the crazy journey with me.

- Juli ~ your magnificent ability to find gems in the craziness of my thoughts will forever astound me; you made my words come to life.

- Joey ~ in one conversation, you changed everything, I adore you.

- Nido ~ you are my role model of intentional attention. Your impact and influence has a rippple effect across the planet.

If you have made it all the end of
this indulgent thank-you list, yay you!

Don't wait for a project like this, or a life-changing
situation to remind someone they mean something to
you. Take a moment today, make a call, send a text,
write a love note, call a customer to thank them, and
reach out to someone and acknowledge the impact
they make or have made on you.

Let's pay more
attention together.

When you pay attention, attention pays.

♡ —Neen James

About the Author

Think force of nature. Boundless energy. Dubbed the *Energizer bunny* by event planners worldwide, she's a highly rated keynote speaker and sassy little Aussie. With a down-to-earth style, contagious enthusiasm, and sharp business mind, Neen has also authored three books including Folding Time™ and contributed to four books. She is a regular contributor to industry publications and online forums, as well as a sought-after thought leader in productivity and attention.

Her company provides high-energy keynotes and executive mentoring. Clients describe her as fun, real, energetic, and wicked smart. Neen is happily married, a self-proclaimed champagne taste tester, shoe-loving, proud godmother of Maddie and Ava.

Learn more at neenjames.com.

Introduction

DOES YOUR ATTENTION PAY?

Are you tired of constantly being busy but not productive?

Do you run from one meeting to the next, yet never feel like you achieve results?

Do you feel overwhelmed, overstressed, and overtired?

Are your personal and professional lives suffering because you can't devote quality time and attention to either?

If you answered yes to any of these questions, you're not alone.

For more than 15 years, I've worked with leaders and professionals in a multitude of industries. Almost every client I work with lists these same concerns within minutes of our first meeting. They all have something else in common, too—the desire to move past their overwhelmed, overstressed, and overtired existence and lead a more fulfilled, productive, and intentional life.

Do you want that, too?

I think most of us do. Yet that possibility seems forever out of reach in a world that constantly demands more from us. It's frustrating when we feel like we work so hard to create a lifestyle for the people we love, and yet we aren't getting enough time with those we care about.

Many clients share with me that they don't feel valued at work, and some share they feel the same at home. That makes my heart sad. I want to fix that, and that is the driving force behind my work and this book.

My clients also tell me they simply don't have enough time in the day to "get it all done." Can you relate? If so, I will give you the same tough love I give my clients:

You don't have a time management crisis; you have an attention management crisis.

In my work, I show leaders how to be highly productive and achieve lasting work-life integration. (I don't believe in the work-life balance myth! More on that later.) It seems there is one fundamental characteristic that too many of today's leaders are lacking: the ability to give their undivided attention to whom and what matters most at that moment.

I'm not talking half-hearted, kinda listening, multitasking, doing something on your phone attention. I mean deliberate, fully present, look-them-in-the-eye type of attention.

I see this same attention crisis everywhere I look—in our homes, in our workplaces, in our communities. We think we're paying attention but we're not. As individuals, professionals, and communities, our genuine engagement has dramatically declined. Our attention is being wasted—stolen by technology, constant interruptions, and our own habits.

We have become an attention-deficit society.

We now accept *distracted* as the norm. We are so focused on technology, our never-ending to-do list, and our lack of time, we fail to pay attention to the people, priorities, and passions that are truly important to us. We are more connected than any time in history and yet more disconnected from ourselves, from each other, from our work, and from our world than ever before.

You know what I am talking about. I know you see it, too. No one truly pays attention anymore.

THE COSTS OF INATTENTION

You might be sitting there thinking, "Really? Attention? Is it that important?"

Yeah, actually it is.

As you'll discover in Chapter 1, the cost of our inattention is real and the consequences are enormous. And I don't mean just financial costs. There are tangible personal, professional, and societal costs to our individual and collective lack of attention.

At a personal level, our health, our relationships, and our opportunities for career advancement suffer significantly when we don't give thoughtful attention to ourselves and the people we care about most. Professionally, lack of attention has a dramatic negative impact on our productivity, employee engagement, sales, and bottom-line results. Globally, our carelessness has led to irreparable harm to our natural resources, plant and animal species, and the planet itself.

The price we are paying for our inattention is far too great.

You get just one life to lead. How do you want to spend that life? Overwhelmed, overstressed, and overtired? Or joyful, productive, and attentive? Are you squandering the amazing talents and skills you possess because you can't stay focused at work? We have only one planet to care for. What kind of legacy and world are we leaving to our grandchildren?

You may think you are paying attention, but are you giving *intentional attention*? You may think you are doing work that matters, but maybe you're not. You may think you make people feel like they matter, but do they really?

It's not that we don't want to pay attention. We really are trying.

- We believe *connecting* with friends and family through social media creates authentic, meaningful connections.

- We think survival by multitasking is our only option.
- We are trying to be all things to all people.
- We feel that we have to be accessible to everyone all the time.
- We create mindfulness programs at work.
- We go to time-management training programs.
- We create never-ending to-do lists.
- We spend more time prioritizing our to-do lists than actually doing our to-do lists!
- We try new fancy planners.
- We download the latest app.
- We color code our calendars.
- We read anything we can get our hands on about how to get it all done.

And yet, we still feel frustrated.

We are missing something when it comes to understanding attention.

INTENTION IS WHAT MAKES ATTENTION VALUABLE

Have you ever thought about the value of paying attention?

Attention sometimes gets a bad rap in today's society. Perhaps that is because we've come to associate the concept of attention with unrelenting selfies that scream *look at me* and the constant sharing of every detail of one's life on social media. That is not the type of attention I am talking about. The type of attention I want to share with you in this book is the *intentional attention* that will help you show up as the best version of yourself in all roles in your life.

We all want and need attention. It's one of our most basic human desires. From our earliest moments as infants, our most basic needs of food, shelter and nurturing are provided by our parents' attention. As adults, the love and acceptance we all crave is granted by others' attention to us.

We don't all need the same kind of attention. It doesn't even have to be a lot of attention—just attention from the people who are important to us. We want to feel that we are the center of somebody's attention, even if we don't want to be the center of everybody's attention.

Attention is critical in our jobs, too. We need focused attention from our leaders and our employees to get work done, to achieve results, to succeed. Our customers and our teams need attention, too. People want to be seen and heard and know that their concerns are being addressed.

Attention is not optional; it's vital. *It is attention that drives the results we all want and need.*

Perhaps this is why we hear all the time, "Pay attention!" Our parents told us to pay attention. Our teachers told us to pay attention. We tell our kids to pay attention. It's a valuable life lesson.

The issue is that most of us are giving distracted, unfocused attention (like texting while having a conversation). That kind of attention is worthless. It sends the message that the focus of our attention has little real value, meaning, or importance to us.

Intention *is what makes* attention *valuable.*

Intentional attention is active. It involves seeing, hearing, and thinking about who is with you and what needs your focus right now. It requires us to choose consciously, act deliberately, and invest transformationally with our attention. That is the essence of Attention Pays—*intentionally investing your attention in what matters at the moment: the people you are talking to, the priorities you are acting on, and the passions you are pursuing.*

Just as you must first invest your money before you can expect any return, you have to first give attention in order to receive the benefits. We have to give attention to get attention. How can you manage and invest your attention so that it pays? That is the question we are going to answer in this book.

Now before you start thinking this is a narcissistic, hedonistic book about how you can manipulate others to get what you want, just stop. Attention Pays is not about giving to get. Giving others the authentic, deliberate attention they need is transformational—for them and for you. When you meet others' needs, yours will naturally be met, too.

When you give the people, priorities, and passions in your life your undivided attention, in the moment, you reap lasting rewards. When companies give attention first to their team members, clients, and customers, they get the attention they want and need for their products and services. This is not because they are trying to manipulate, but because they stand out among their competitors. And when we give the planet our committed attention, we ensure it will take care of us in the future.

Intentional attention is a gift—one you give the people in your world, and one you give yourself.

AN ATTENTION REVOLUTION

Through my research, study, and work with clients such as Viacom, Comcast, Paramount Pictures, Trinity Health, and Johnson & Johnson Pharmaceuticals, I've seen the power of intentional attention. I've repeatedly witnessed firsthand the extraordinary difference even slight shifts in attention can create in people's lives. That is why the concept of intentional attention is the underpinning of my business practice, my strategy development, and my passion for helping people get from where they are to where they want to be.

My personal mission is to dismantle our attention-deficit society and create an attention-surplus economy.

I want the world to stop the "crazy" and pay attention to each other and create more significant moments that matter.

I want to inspire an Attention Revolution to help each of us to move past busyness into productiveness, to make genuine connections and deepen our relationships, to accelerate results and to achieve lasting work–life integration.

I want you to look up at the magnificent world around you and really notice people. I want you to take a moment and look someone deeply in the eyes. I want you to pause, take a breath, and be right here in this very moment.

I want everyone to feel seen and heard. I don't want anyone to ever feel invisible.

Will you join me?

As an executive, leader, parent, business owner, coach, entrepreneur, board member, or all the other roles you fill each day, you can choose how you will invest your attention, time, and energy:

- *Personally—Be Thoughtful* as an individual.

- *Professionally—Be Productive* as an individual and leader.

- *Globally—Be Responsible* for your community and your world.

Together, let's create an Attention Revolution so that those you spend time with at work, home, and in your community will know that they matter to you.

ATTENTION PAYS

Intentional attention is like currency. When you invest it wisely, it pays meaningful, long-term dividends. By intentionally and deliberately paying attention to who and what matters, we get the results we want at work, at home, and in our communities. Might it be difficult? You bet! But the ROA—*return on attention*—is huge!

One of the biggest returns on your intentional attention is the creation of truly defining moments, not just for you, but for others. My wish for you is that you design a life filled with significant moments you will remember, share, and celebrate and that those moments will include the people you love at home and the people you care for at work. I want you to be proud of your successes and create experiences in the world you will never forget.

> ### How Well Does *Your* Attention Pay?
>
> Find out right now by taking our quick, free online questionnaire at neenjames.com/extras

Creating significant moments is just the start. Intentional attention pays in so many other ways.

Personally

- Deepen relationships
- Achieve work–life integration
- Find greater purpose and meaning
- Create more meaningful memories
- Increase wealth

Professionally

- Create laser focus
- Boost productivity
- Accelerate results
- Increase profitability

- Enhance accountability
- Grow client/customer base and sales
- Improve client/customer satisfaction and loyalty
- Enrich team dynamics and improve morale
- Attract and retain top talent
- Get promoted
- Heighten employee engagement

Globally
- Spread respect and kindness for others
- Protect vital resources
- Honor our environment
- Leave a lasting legacy

We all have responsibilities at work, home, and in our community to pay attention. How well does your attention pay?

ATTENTION IS YOGA FOR YOUR MIND

Why is it that despite the fact we've been told from childhood to pay attention, we still haven't figured it out? It's not that we aren't smart. It's that so many other things are constantly competing for our attention, and all that competition leads to endless distractions and interruptions.

This book will show you how to change your focus, change your habits, and change your brain so you can pay attention to what matters and make your attention pay. You'll learn how to be intentional with who gets your attention, be productive in what gets your attention, and be responsible for the impact of your attention. I'll give you specific strategies that you can put to use immediately at work and at home. You'll discover how these strategies have paid off for other leaders like you. And of course, we will have fun chatting along the way, and you will learn way more about me than maybe even my mum knows. (Yes, that's how we spell *mum* in Australia—before any of you want to let me know there is a spelling error in my book!)

I can't change your brain, but you can. That might mean you need to stop some of your behaviors. It might mean you will feel uncomfortable reading through some suggestions. But my wish for you is that you will find new ways to not just pay attention, but also to aspire to attentiveness.

By the time you finish this book (if you make it all the way to the end), you will be more intentional with your attention—*if* you are willing to put in some effort. Every. Single. Day. Intentional attention is a skill you can build just like you build a muscle, but it takes practice.

Have you ever done yoga? If so, have you heard the instructor say, "Yoga is a daily practice." Think of attention as yoga for your mind. Intentional attention is a deliberate, daily practice. The more you do it, the better you get at it. And it's so worth it. How do I know? Because like you, attention is a daily practice for me. I am a work in progress. The only difference is that maybe I have been practicing a bit longer than you.

We need to come to the mat each day, ready to work with the body and mind we have, to get the strength we need to achieve great things.

Let's choose to truly pay attention to what matters so we can be happier in our relationships, more fulfilled in the work we do, and safer in the world we have created. This way we can create meaning, create success, and create a legacy.

Let's pay more attention together. Ready?

PART ONE

Does Your Attention Pay?

CHAPTER 1

Our Attention-Deficit Society

Have you ever heard someone say, "I have ADD today"?

ADD (attention-deficit disorder) has become a catchphrase for laziness, often used as an excuse for procrastination, lack of productivity, being easily distracted, not paying attention, and not completing tasks. People seem to wear it like a badge of honor, which is odd if you think about it.

ADD and ADHD (attention-deficit/hyperactivity disorder) are true disorders that require medical treatment. They are physiological, biochemical disorders that make it hard for a person to stay focused and pay attention, thus limiting their ability to perform to their full potential.

When I say that we have become an *attention-deficit society*, I don't say it lightly. One of my family members was diagnosed with ADD in 1992, and I have seen the impacts of this firsthand. But I use this phrase intentionally to drive the point home that there is an epidemic of inattention in our

world—a widespread, serious condition that has real consequences. Consider the following:

- Nine people die every day and 1,153 people are injured
  because of distracted driving. These are not just name-
  less, faceless people. These are partners, mothers, fathers,
  children, siblings, and friends. Possibly yours.

- The death count of pedestrians in Minneapolis, Min-
  nesota, is steadily rising due to distracted walking. They
  have a light rail system, and people are so absorbed with
  their cell phones they don't even see a train coming at
  them!

- According to a study by the Information Overload
  Group, $588 billion is lost every year in U.S. businesses
  alone because of interruptions.

- In a study of 2,000 respondents, *Think Money* found a
  total of 759 hours (that's 31 days!) in lost time every year
  due to distractions.

- Since the year 1900, about 477 different species have
  become extinct because of our inattention to our environment and the destruction of natural habitats.

- The Global Nonrenewable Natural Resource Scarcity
  Assessment found that 23 of the 26 (88%) nonrenewable natural resources it analyzed will likely experience
  permanent global supply shortfalls by the year 2030.

Our inattention has real, often lasting, and sometimes devastating consequences. We think we are paying attention, but
we aren't. We are allowing other people, devices, and circumstances to control our attention.

Those with true ADD don't have a choice in how well
they pay attention. The rest of us do. We don't have ADD; we
have IBC—*inattention by choice*. We have control of our brains,

our thought processes, and our habits. Stop thinking that you have no power over your inattention and lack of productivity. Nothing could be further from the truth.

So, how did we get here? How did we become an attention-deficit society?

It's not because we're not smart or because we don't care, but because so many other things are competing for our attention, both online and offline. The causes of the attention-deficit society are both internal and external forces. Our fast paced, device-dependent, hyperconnected world is speeding up, not slowing down. We have so many distractions and decisions, we can't focus in the moment for a minute.

Let's take a closer look at each of these internal and external factors.

INTERNAL FACTORS

Our internal world is a significant factor in our struggle to pay attention. Our beliefs, our feelings, our health, and even our generation play a role in how well we pay attention.

The Great Multitasking Myth

In our modern world, the number of things that demand our attention has dramatically increased. We are being pulled in so many different directions and being asked to produce better results faster and with fewer resources. Our solution has been to multitask or *manic-task*, as I call it. I've been guilty of this—frantically switching between screens, paper, calls, and to-do lists in an attempt to get it all done.

For years, we've been told that multitasking was the way to be more efficient and productive. Too bad it's not true. The reality is we are multitasking more yet achieving less. We are busy, but not productive. We still feel like we can't get it all done. Don't you feel that? And it's stressful, right?

The idea that multitasking will help us get more done is a myth. As a result of numerous studies and neuroscience research, we now know that the brain is incapable of performing multiple tasks simultaneously (yes, including talking and texting). Rather than multitasking, the brain is rapidly shifting from one task to another. And each time the brain switches tasks, it has to go through a start-stop-start process. Some estimates suggest that productivity goes down by as much as 40% to 50% when we task switch. Other studies have found that because this task switching increases the cognitive load on our brains, it also increases the chances of making mistakes and missing important information and cues, as well as hinders problem solving and creativity.

In his book *Free*, Chris Anderson, founder of TED Talks and editor-in-chief of *Wired* magazine, asked the reader, "Does multitasking just slice the same attention more finely?"

The answer is *yes*. We are splitting our attention in many different directions, giving a piece of our attention here, a piece there, and another piece over there. As a result, nothing is getting our true attention and everything is getting short-changed. We need to replace our manic-tasking with single-tasking or *sane-tasking*, as I call it—staying sane while focusing our attention on the important conversation, proposal, or project at hand until it is completed.

Which do *you* do more of—manic-tasking or sane-tasking?

The "Over Trilogy"—Overwhelmed, Overstressed, and Overtired

I imagine you are a high achiever. You want more, you hustle, you want to be at the top, have the best team, achieve the president's award, or get a fantastic rating on your annual performance review. You want it all. Many of us do. But that leads to a dangerous condition that I call the "Over Trilogy"—the fact

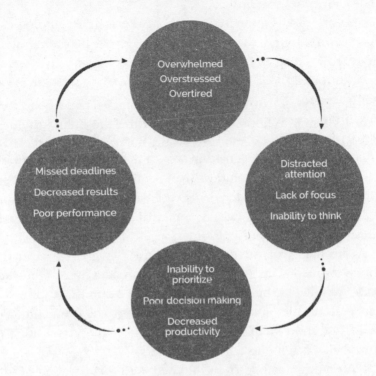

Figure 1.1. The Over Trilogy Cycle

that too many of us are constantly overwhelmed, overstressed, and overtired.

We feel constantly overwhelmed as our responsibilities at work and at home continue to grow. We attempt to answer emails between meetings, eat on the run living on protein bars, create some structure for our teams, respond to the boss, and then look after our family. Our boss has expectations of us, our partners have different expectations, and then we have expectations of ourselves about what we can achieve. We want so much more in life, but we don't know where to begin.

If you are like most of the leaders I work with, you are more stressed than ever before. And you're not alone.

A recent study conducted by the American Psychological Association found that average stress levels in the United States rose yet again from 4.9 to 5.1 on a 10-point stress scale. In addition, 24% of adults reported being extremely stressed, compared to 18% a year earlier.

Chronic stress impairs our ability to shift our attention. A 2009 study of stressed-out medical students found that stress affects the attention-regulating area of the prefrontal cortex of the brain. The study's author shared, "It's reassuring that this attention-shifting deficit seems to go away after the stress is reduced, but such deficits are similar to what we see in some stress-related psychiatric disorders."

More than that, stress is a silent killer. We can't see it or touch it or smell it. But we can see the impacts of it. Chronic stress is linked to the six leading causes of death (heart disease, cancer, lung ailments, accidents, cirrhosis of the liver, and suicide), and more than 75% of all physician office visits are for stress-related ailments and complaints.

Constantly feeling overwhelmed and overstressed leads to being overtired. Too many of us (yes, I'm guilty of it, too) are living an around-the-clock schedule, staying up too late or getting up too early in a futile effort to get it all done. Chronic lack of sleep impacts our mental alertness, productivity, attitude, and emotions. But it can also lead to serious medical conditions and shorten life expectancy.

Even if we make it into the bed at a reasonable hour, how often do we lie in bed tossing and turning, letting overwhelm and overstress take over our minds? I often refer to the overwhelm and overstress combination as *Chip*, like a chip on your shoulder (apologies to my friend whose real name is Chip). I think of Chip as this vicious green gremlin who visits late at night. He taunts you relentlessly, reminding you of everything you didn't get done today. He's ugly, and he distracts you.

What does the Over Trilogy have to do with attention? Everything! Being overwhelmed, overstressed, and overtired impacts our health and our relationships. A constant level of overwhelm, stress, and fatigue deeply affects our attention and takes up valuable real estate in our brain, thus negatively impacting the way our brain processes information. This leads to decreased productivity and eventually decreased results, which triggers even more feelings of being overwhelmed, overstressed, and overtired. The result is a never-ending, vicious cycle.

It's time to punch Chip in the face, tell him he's not welcome, and decide that you are done being overwhelmed, overstressed, and overtired. It's no way to live. Instead, choose to live a meaningful life filled with significant moments.

Generational Differences

I speak to a lot of people every year. People think I can't see them in the audience because of the lights, but I can. In fact, I make it a habit to observe whether my audience members are paying attention to me. (The responsibility is on me, the speaker, to keep them engaged. The same is true for any speaker, or any leader for that matter.) I've noticed some differences that seem to run along generational lines. You would likely notice the same differences if you observed the audience at your CEO's annual presentation or groups of friends sitting around tables at a restaurant.

The older generations will put their devices away and look at the speaker or at each other. Now, that doesn't mean they are paying attention! They could be thinking about problems at work, problems at home, what they're going to say next, or running through the to-do lists in their head.

The younger generations have their phones out, typing away, perhaps tweeting a great quote from the CEO, or posting a picture of their entrée. Older generations tend to believe younger generations are being rude when they are on their phones in the company of others. Younger generations would never be offended by someone being on a phone in their presence. They are just excited to spread the latest news, whatever that may be.

Both older and younger generations likely think they are paying attention. Both probably aren't.

But their perceptions of their own and others' attention are very different. Those who grew up before the advent of the internet and smartphone likely know how to give someone undivided attention, how to be present in the moment during a special event, or how to focus on a task for more than a few minutes. But like any good skill, if you don't use it, you lose it. Those who grew up in the digital age have never known anything other than a multitasking, multiscreen, always-connected existence.

The youngest generation is growing up on a full-time diet of technology, electronics, and social media almost from the time they are infants. Their babysitters are watching movies on a tablet and playing games on smartphones. According to a study performed by the International Center for Media & the Public Agenda, most children and teens spend 75% of their waking lives with their eyes fixed on a screen. It remains to be seen if their brains will actually be wired differently than the brains of older generations. In the meantime, we know the brain can't do two things at once.

I recently had a conversation with my incredibly talented 21-year-old neighbor about attention and his generation. He said when his generation meets with people who are older than them, they don't tend to be on their devices out of respect. (Except with their parents—they think that's very different.) It was fascinating. That tells me that, despite what younger generations tell us about their ability to pay attention to more than one thing at time, deep down they know it isn't true.

Whichever generation you resonate with, we need to understand not all generations see attention the same way as us. Let's focus on how we can be better at paying attention, regardless of the generation to which we belong.

EXTERNAL FACTORS

Our beliefs, thoughts, feelings, and even our age affect our ability to pay attention. But our inattention is not just an inside job. There are external influences that compromise our attention, as well.

Physical Environment

If you are sitting at your desk right now, look up. Take a good look around you. Do you have paper everywhere? Big piles of things to do? A full physical inbox of projects needing your input, journals that need reading, or proposals that need responding to? When you look at your computer screen, do you have a huge email inbox that you use as your to-do list?

When you arrive home after work, can you park your car in your garage? Or is the space filled with boxes and projects and reminders of things you *have to do*?

Our physical environment affects our ability to achieve results. If it feels out of control, disorganized, and chaotic, we are less likely to know where to focus first.

Open-plan environments are another physical factor that can dramatically impact our attention and productivity. Open-plan environments are popular and beneficial for teams with high collaboration, and allow a larger number of people in one space. Many successful organizations have moved to this model including Facebook, Cisco, Microsoft, Google, and eBay.

While companies will not go back to offices any time soon, we need to understand as leaders that an open-plan environment creates massive distractions for all team members and impacts productivity negatively. Their attention will be split, their phone calls will be heard, their sales will be affected, and team morale will be impacted.

You can make open-plan work only with training, guidelines, and old-fashioned good manners and thoughtful team members.

Visit neenjames.com to download my free 10-Day Open Plan Productivity Action Plan and Open Plan Survival Tips.

The Survival Tips can be found directly at neenjames.com/extras.

How the Media and Information Overload Changed Our Attention

If you didn't pay attention as a caveman or cave woman, you just might get eaten by a saber-toothed tiger or pick the wrong berries to eat. That was good incentive to know what was happening around you. Paying attention was critical to survival. Fortunately for our early ancestors, they didn't have TV and other modern technologies to distract them!

Over time, people began to multiply, explore new areas, and build and live in larger communities. With the invention of tools and resources to make people's lives easier, attention shifted from survival to communication, trade, and learning about the world.

Just 80 years ago, families stopped what they were doing to gather around the radio to hear the news that was impacting their world. With limited information, everyone gave that information their undivided attention.

With the invention of the television, our world exponentially expanded, but information was still generally limited to one daily print edition of the newspaper and a few daily television newscasts. When I was a child, TV was a treat. It had a place in our home, but it wasn't on all day. When my husband and I got married, we didn't own a TV for the first two years and we loved that. We made a conscious choice not to have a television; newlyweds have far more interesting things to do!

Today, with almost unlimited cable and satellite channels, people can tune into the news—or any other channel for that matter—24 hours a day. I have stayed with friends at their homes (or even sharing a hotel room) and the first thing they do when they wake up is turn on the TV. Now, we eat with the TV or phone or other device instead of with people.

When Netflix began creating shows that allowed every episode to be available at once (instead of waiting from one week to the next), we changed our viewing habits. Binge-watching is one of the latest ways media steals our attention. The Diffusion Group (TDG) published research findings on exstreamist.com that we spend more time watching Netflix than eating, reading, or having sex!

But that's not the end of it. Now, we get our news and entertainment through screens and apps on our devices. We can google anything and there is a YouTube video for how to do everything. I heard the news that Michael Jackson died on Twitter. I often learn about world events on Facebook posts or tweets from those in affected areas. Social media has changed the way we receive breaking news; it has created millions of unofficial journalists sharing stories from all over the world and it has created skeptical viewers now that *fake news* has become a real issue.

According to Adrian Ott, one of Silicon Valley's most respected strategists and the author of the book *The 24-Hour Customer*, we see more than 34 billion bits of information per day online. That is the equivalent of two books a day! And all that information creates pressure on what she calls *the attention bottleneck*—the imbalance between the rate of information growth relative to the fixed constraint of time. She explains,

> In 16 waking hours a day, people can only comprehend a finite amount of what's thrown at them. The information coming into the top of the funnel is growing at an increasing rate while the intake at the bottom remains fixed, adding pressure to the attention bottleneck . . . . This dynamic has driven an attention arms race where it feels like we are in Times Square with lights flashing and noise blaring all the time, no matter where we are. The kind of discipline required to shut out the world and avoid multitasking with all the electronic temptations at our fingertips is significantly greater than in the past.

In addition, advertisers have become incredibly savvy at manipulating our attention. Leveraging technology that measures brain activity and heart rate, as well as tracks eyeballs to see what colors, messages, and images cause emotional reactions, they can design campaigns that get and keep our attention.

Our exposure to choices and information is much greater than in our parents' time. With information overload, it seems no one pays much attention to anything. Herbert Simon, a social scientist in 1971, said, "A wealth of information creates a poverty of attention." Wise words.

Our Technology Addiction

Have you ever been at a wedding (or even worse, a funeral) and heard a cell phone ring? I don't care who you are or what message someone is trying to get to you. Nothing about this is okay.

In our attention-deficit society, we have become hyper-focused on our smartphones, smart devices, social media, and text messaging, rather than on who or what is important in the moment. We have made technology more important than people.

My talented friend and sales and leadership speaker Connie Podesta shared a story with me. She and a friend had agreed to meet but only had 60 minutes due to their busy schedules. When the time was over, the friend had spent 50% of that time on her cell phone and responding to messages. Her friend lamented their time had come to an end but commented on how good it had been to catch up. My brave and fabulous friend Connie replied, "It would have been nice to catch up, but you spent half the time on your phone."

We have all come to accept people being on devices while in conversation as normal and acceptable. It's not! We need more people like Connie—willing to point out the truth about our obsession with our devices and technology. I have been known to say to my honey, "I am more interesting than your phone." It may sound arrogant as you read it, but it's true. I am interesting and it makes him laugh.

Have you ever found yourself reaching for your device if a person, or meeting, or a movie didn't engage you? It's become our default. Our technology and our devices have become our companionship. Here's something scary: The International Center for Media & the Public Agenda found that students who unplugged their electronic devices for one 24-hour period felt extremely lonely and didn't know how to fill their time.

The truth is, we are addicted. And I don't mean figuratively, I mean literally.

Dr. Nicholas Kardaras, author of *Glow Kids: How Screen Addiction Is Hijacking Our Kids—and How to Break the Trance*, says there's a very real reason why it's so hard to coax people away from their devices. "We now know that those iPads, smartphones, and Xboxes are a form of digital drug.

Recent brain imaging research is showing that they affect the brain's frontal cortex—which controls executive functioning, including impulse control—in exactly the same way that cocaine does. Technology is so hyper-arousing that it raises dopamine levels—the feel-good neurotransmitter most involved in the addiction dynamic—as much as sex."

As much as we may not want to admit that we are addicted to our devices, we know we are. Have you ever left the house without your cell phone? Did you go back to get it? Even if it made you late for work or you missed your train? Of course you did!

The idea of a *digital detox* gives some people heart palpitations. Do you know how many times we touch our cell phones in a day? Take a guess.

Think You're Not Addicted to Technology?

There are numerous apps available that track how much time you spend on your smartphone. You can leverage technology to actually help your attention. Install one and see how much time you are really spending on your phone. I installed one and was shocked at how much time I was wasting on my device. This dependency on our technology is impacting our relationships and our performance. Imagine what your life would be like if you gave the people, priorities, and passions that are important to you half of the attention you give your devices! Do you want to write a book? Imagine if you added to it 2,617 times a day. Imagine what you could achieve if you invested only a third of that time developing a new skill you want to develop?

Go to neenjames.com/extras for my favorite Attention Resources.

According to a recent Dscout study, the average user touches their cell phone 2,617 time per day! Imagine touching anything—or anyone—that many times a day! If you are an extreme user—someone who is never separated from your device—you might touch your cell phone over 5,400 times per day! That's just crazy!

Now, you might think that I believe technology is the evil enemy of attention. Not at all. Technology is an amazing tool that has become an integral part of societal change. It gets blamed (a lot) for our lack of attention, but when leveraged well, it can help us achieve more in shorter periods of time and create a further reach than we ever thought possible.

But we have willingly given away our power and our control to our devices. We have allowed our devices to dictate our time and our attention, and therefore our lives.

We haven't figure out how to deal with technology's incessant demand on our attention. We haven't learned how to use technology appropriately and still be productive and so our attention is devoured online. We haven't designed the rules or taught people how to behave in the digital age with manners and respect.

Technology, when used wisely, can increase attention and productivity and connectivity. Like any good thing, using technology in moderation is a powerful tool for all of us. We need to leverage technology, not reject it. We need to be disciplined in our use of technology, especially while in the company of the people around us. The key is to use it for good (productivity), and not evil (pure distraction). We get to choose our relationship with technology. We can reclaim our time and attention, and this book will show you exactly how to do this.

Our Addiction to Social Media and Apps

The first tweet by one of the Twitter founders, Jack Dorsey, sent on March 21, 2006, at 9:50 p.m. read, "just setting up my twttr." This one action forever changed the status updates for social media. When Twitter launched in July of that year, they could not have begun to imagine the far-reaching impact they would have on the world's attention.

Twitter and all its social media cousins have become part of our daily attention and conversation—and our obsession. Our addiction to our technology is driven largely by our addiction to social media and apps.

Apps and social media are stealing our attention. We have become obsessed with likes, and retweets, and finding the perfect *gif* response to post. We miss the amazing play or moment at the concert because we are updating our Instagram. We miss the bus because we are enthralled with the latest video on one of our YouTube subscriptions. We miss our floor on the elevator because we were reading Twitter. We miss the green light because we are checking Facebook.

The CEO of a technology and data company recently shared with me his frustration about one of his senior leaders who appeared to be addicted to Candy Crush. In every spare moment, his director was online and had to be counseled twice in one week. The leader tried to explain it was his form of relaxation but after much questioning, he reluctantly admitted that his workload had fallen behind, he had emails in his inbox that hadn't been answered for five days, and he was two weeks behind in developing a database for a client. Remember, this is a smart, functioning adult.

Maybe you don't play Candy Crush but you feel a need to check every notification of a new email, text, tweet, or post on

Facebook or LinkedIn, or maybe you have created Pinterest boards to plan your perfectly designed office or maybe you monitor every like you get on Instagram?

Gut check time: How much of *your* attention is being stolen by apps and social media?

Do we really have to include in our employee policies that people can't play Candy Crush or check social media at work? Possibly. Some of our obsession is driven by habit and some of it by boredom. And it could be that the voyeuristic interest in other people's lives is more exciting than whatever work is in front of us.

But there is more to it than that. The addiction is real. Our impulse to play one more game and check social media is driven by dopamine and the reward center of the brain. A recent study conducted by researchers at Harvard University found that sharing information about ourselves on social media activates the same part of the brain that is associated with the sensation of pleasure, the same pleasure that we get from eating food, getting money, or having sex. Researchers also learned that there is even greater activity in the reward center of the brain when we share our thoughts with family or friends.

People are addicted to likes and other *vanity metrics* (a term coined by Eric Ries, author of the book *The Lean Start-Up*). "It's an endless pursuit of vanity metrics that stroke the ego," says speaker and author of *UnMarketing*, Scott Stratten.

Another factor in our addiction is FOMO—Fear of Missing Out. We have to be on this or that social media network because "everybody" is on this or that social media network. What if we aren't up to date on what our friends are talking about? What if we miss out on the latest news? Even people who don't like social media feel compelled to join because that's where all of their family, friends, and colleagues are spending their time.

Technology and social media companies and app developers also very consciously and intentionally feed our addictions. Tristan Harris, a former Google design ethicist and an executive at Time Well Spent, believes advertisers and these companies are hijacking our brains. He's passionate about this topic. Harris shares that companies are investing millions of dollars in app, screen design, incentives, and advertisements to get and keep our attention.

Mike Elgan, technology and tech culture columnist at *ComputerWorld*, believes, "Social networking is engineered to be as habit-forming as crack cocaine." He points out that social media sites become more addictive every day through developer strategies like notification numbers, click bait, and algorithmic filters: " . . . the sites are in a war for survival where only the most addictive sites will survive. Meanwhile, our innate human ability to resist this addiction doesn't evolve."

I can hear you now: "Neen, social media and technology allow me to connect with more people more often." In Australia, we have a saying: "Rubbish!" (the equivalent of *bull*★★★★). Let's get real. Liking a friend from high school's vacation picture or responding with an emoji to the news of a death in a former coworker's family is not a real connection.

I'm not trying to bash social media. It can be a powerful way to show someone attention. I give lots of *intentional* attention to family, friends, colleagues, and clients on Facebook and other platforms. It also allows me to connect to my family in Australia, chat with friends around the world, and witness life-changing events for others in real time.

But love it or hate it, there is no denying that social media demands our attention. While we scroll through Facebook, scroll through Instagram stories, and scroll through Twitter, we are mindlessly scrolling through our lives. I doubt anyone will say on their deathbed, "I wish I'd posted one more tweet or picture." But sadly, they just might say, "I wish I'd paid more attention to the people I was with rather than the ones on social media."

Destruction of the Work-Life Boundary

Many of you reading this book are too young to remember the "old days" when you arrived at your workplace, went to an office, sat at your desk, and looked in your physical inbox where you had a pile of papers that were your tasks to be completed for that day. As a task was completed, it went in the physical outbox or was distributed throughout your organization via a written memo placed in mailboxes in a mailroom. Once your inbox was empty, your work was done and you went home. I know. Sounds crazy, right?

In your personal time, you exercised, pursued hobbies, spent time with your family or friends, ate around the dinner table, and went to your kids' activities—where you actually paid attention and connected with other parents. You could answer truthfully when your child asked if you saw their big moment. You might occasionally have taken some work or work-related reading home, but there were very clear boundaries between what happened at work and what happened at home. We respected office hours.

And then technology changed our lives. We began using systems like email and instant message, and then pagers. Cell phones, originally purchased for some to make us feel safe or for use in an emergency, made us available to just about anyone at any time of the day or night. Our technology created a prison of sorts. We are now trapped by our accessibility.

We have moved from very clear boundaries between work and home to being always "on." The 9-to-5 has become 24/7, 365. We have stopped respecting boundaries and time zones. We email at all times of the day and night. We respond to work requests on weekends. We call in to conference calls when we are on vacation. We watch our kids play sports and sit in on teleconferences. No wonder we are overwhelmed, overstressed, and overtired.

The lines between work life and personal life are blurred, if not gone altogether. We check social media, text messages, and personal email during work hours. We answer work emails during our supposed off time at home, on weekends, and on vacation. The old adage *Leave work at work and home at home*, is a joke.

There was a fundamental shift in the work-life boundary that occurred not long after the smartphone began to get smart. Employers allow employees to work late, work on the weekends, and work slowly the whole time. Leadership has unrealistic expectations that employees should be constantly available. According to the U.S. Travel Association, nearly 20% of managers feel employees who take all earned leave are less dedicated and focused in their jobs. And employees fear their jobs won't be there when they return from a break.

The destruction of the work-life boundary is a huge factor in our attention-deficit society. The problem with always being "on" is that our attention is always constantly split between our work and personal lives. And that means that neither is getting quality attention or quality effort. (Remember the vicious Over Trilogy cycle?, See Figure 1.1)

While technology was the means for the destruction of the work-life boundary, it's not to blame. It's humans that are to blame. We control the tools we use. It's user error. We have to stop the madness!

We all know we can't go back to the old days with a crisp line of demarcation between work and home. The genie is out of the bottle and there is no way he is going back in! But what would happen if we set some boundaries? As organizations, as leaders, and as individuals, we need to make it okay to have rest and recovery periods and to recharge our batteries. We need to make it okay to pay attention to what really matters at work when we are there and to what really matters at home when we are there. How much more productive could we be if we focused and paid attention to who and what was important at the appropriate time?

Do you recall when it was bad manners to call someone before 9 a.m. and after 9 PM? Did you know about the telemarketing sales law that establishes standards of conduct for telemarketing calls that they can't call you before 8 a.m. or after 9 p.m.? We need to create new rules like this in our organizations. Yes, I'm completely serious. I challenge you to try it and see how much more creative and productive your team becomes.

It's time to stop the insanity and restore some work-life integration. Creating work-life integration is one of the biggest benefits of joining me in my Attention Revolution. You see, I think work-life balance is a myth. Many of us chase work-life balance, and it's like a unicorn; it will never be discovered. The visual of work and life being a set of scales with both sides equal isn't realistic.

I believe in work-life *integration*. What's the difference? Work-life integration is when your environment, emotions, and expectations are what you want them to be. It's creating an environment that works for you. That might mean working from home on a Friday to complete strategic projects.

It's managing your emotions, so you stop feeling guilty about home when you're at work and about work when you're at home. Guilt is a common emotion among executives with whom I work. They feel guilty for staying too long at the office to get things done when they want to be home with their families—the main reason they work as hard as they do. And they feel guilty when they are relaxing on Sunday night with their family knowing their emails are piling up and waiting to be answered.

Work-life integration means managing expectations of yourself and others. There is no prescription; it's wholly designed by you, for you, and where you are in your career and circumstances. Unlike the mythical work-life balance, work-life integration is real, and you can have it.

THE COSTS OF THE ATTENTION-DEFICIT SOCIETY

Every day we waste our attention on inconsequential activities without understanding the consequences of our bad investments. There are huge costs when we don't make the choice to be focused with our attention. We will have big problems personally, professionally, and globally if we allow our attention-deficit society to continue.

Personal Costs
- Death—I'm not trying to be dramatic here; I'm trying to be real. When we don't pay attention while we drive, it kills people. Nine people every day. Think about that for a moment. Nine promising lives gone. Nine families changed forever.

- Our health—The consequences of not paying attention are often stress and illness. There are many people who don't take the time and attention their body needs, or their soul needs. I stupidly ignored a condition for three years, just thinking (or hoping) maybe it would go away, maybe it would fix itself, maybe I was just getting older. Finally, it became so extreme the only solution was surgery. Surgery revealed I'd been putting up with a condition I didn't need to endure. I just didn't stop to take care of it.

- The quality of our relationships—If we do not pay attention to the people who are important to us, they will get their attention somewhere else. One of the reasons for the high rate of divorces and affairs is that people don't feel like they're getting the love and attention they need at home from their partner. So, they go on to find it elsewhere. The cost of sadness and regret are immeasurable.

Professional Costs
- Personal brand—The cost of not paying attention to your personal brand and executive presence could be lost promotions and pay increases and getting passed over for opportunities. If your reputation suffers, you could likely lose influence with your boss, executive leadership, board of directors, or shareholders.

- Customer satisfaction—If you're not listening to your customers, clients, patients, or whomever you serve, they will simply leave and go somewhere else. If you are lucky and they stay, you'll quickly find that their lack of satisfaction leads to increased complaints!

- Productivity—Just because people show up for work physically doesn't mean they are there mentally. When our attention is split, the quality of our work suffers. Interruptions and distractions impact our deliverables and our success rate. It costs significant money to have multiple people in unproductive meetings where little is getting accomplished.

- Team engagement—If you don't take care of your team members, they will leave you to work at another company. In the United States, we lose $11 billion in employee turnover annually according to the Bureau of National Affairs. Paying attention to attracting and retaining your top talent is a wise investment.

- Sales—The cost of not paying attention to your targets (whether you work for an organization or manage your own company) is missed sales opportunities. And we all know what happens when we miss sales goals.

- Profit—When we don't give intentional attention to and in our business, the bottom line suffers. Customer satisfaction, productivity, team engagement, sales—when they drop off, it all falls to the bottom line.

Global Costs

- Resources—Our precious world resources are disappearing, and it's not just fossil fuels and the like. According to Dr. Upmanu Lall, director of the Columbia Water Center and a leading expert on hydroclimatology, as soon as 2025, large parts of the world could experience perennial water shortages. He says, "On a humanitarian level, the possibilities are as devastating as climate change." Many futurists have even theorized the next world war will be fought over water.

- Species—According to Simon Worrall of National Geographic, many people believe that we are in the midst of the sixth mass extinction in Earth's history. The fifth one was when the dinosaurs went extinct. He says, "More species are becoming extinct today than at any time since dinosaurs were wiped off the face of the Earth by an asteroid 65 million years ago. Today we're losing biodiversity at a similar rate. And this is, of course, an anthropogenic mass extinction. The primary cause is human communities." With every species that goes extinct, we not only endanger the future of our own species, but we destroy something very special that our grandchildren and their children will never be able to witness.

- Planet—We need to start paying attention to our planet because we are killing it. There are already so many places in the world that will never be the same. As an Australian, I see the Great Barrier Reef, and it breaks my heart to see how global warming has affected the coral reefs and the marine life that I used to take for granted. It's not just the Great Barrier Reef being devastated by our inattention. Look around the world and where you live and you'll find an example. The rainforests and polar ice caps are just two examples.

To be clear, I am not a card-carrying member of Greenpeace (but I do love some of the work they do), and I don't drive a Tesla (although I love them and think they are incredibly sexy cars). But I am passionate about the fact that we have just one planet, and if we continue to take it for granted, we will all pay the price.

If I haven't convinced you yet that we have an attention management crisis on our hands, I'll save you some time—stop reading. There really is no point in reading any further.

On the other hand, if you see the evidence of the attention-deficit society yourself or you think I might just be on to something here, it's time to join the Attention Revolution. Do you really want to just *exist* in an attention-deficit society? Help me start the shift from the attention-deficit society to the *attention-surplus economy*. It doesn't require a huge investment of time or money. It requires us to make a choice. The choice is to be intentional with who, what, and how we spend our attention. We can change this today. Right now. Read on.

Make Your Attention Pay

1. What do you need to change in your physical environment to improve your attention?
2. Do you have a technology addiction you need to address?
3. What work boundaries do you need to set to improve your work–life integration?

CHAPTER 2

Listen with Your Eyes: The Power of Intentional Attention

"Ms. Neen, do you like Obi Wan or Yoda better?"

"Yoda, of course!" I said.

I was sitting at my next-door neighbor Eileen's kitchen table, savoring a cup of strong, black coffee. Eileen had stepped out of the room, and I had reached for my phone to quickly check email. In Eileen's absence, her five-year-old son Donovan, dressed in his Superman costume, had picked up the conversation with a barrage of questions.

"Ms. Neen, do you like to play outside or inside?"

"Outside."

"Ms. Neen, cats or dogs?"

"Cats," I mumbled.

"MS. NEEN, PAY ATTENTION TO ME—*PLEASE*!"

Startled, I looked up. "I am, honey."

He assured me I was not, stamped his little feet, jumped up in my lap, took my phone out of my hands, and put it on the table. Then he took my face in his tiny little hands and turned it toward him. With great superhero passion and intensity, he said the words I will never forget:

"Pay attention to *me*! Listen with your eyes!"

In that precious moment, Donovan helped me realize why it's so important that we give intentional attention to the people, priorities, and passions that are important to us. It took a five-year-old to teach me the value of truly paying attention and to show me that paying attention is not a passive activity.

Have you ever felt like Donovan?

Have you ever walked into your boss's office to discuss an important issue, but they just keep working on their computer while you are talking to them? Have you ever been in a conversation with someone (perhaps your significant other or one of your kids), and they can't wait for you to finish talking so they can add their two cents? Have you ever been at dinner with a loved one or friend who spends half of the evening answering messages on their phone? It's not a good feeling, is it?

Have you ever been the other person?

Have you ever been the *think you're paying attention but really aren't paying attention* person? Or the person who pretends to be listening when you're actually trying to answer emails and plan your shopping list in your head?

I'll admit it. I've been that person, which is why Donovan's words struck me to the core. They made me reflect on how I was—or wasn't—giving attention to the people, priorities, and passions that were important in my life.

I began observing my colleagues and clients—those who were successful and those who had great potential but struggled to realize that potential and the differences between them. I studied the concept of attention and how much our inattention is costing us personally, professionally, and globally. I spoke with experts and real-world leaders.

I noticed that there are negative connotations about attention in our self-serving world, from people who want their 15 minutes of fame to our obsession with social media. I wanted to focus on the positive aspects of attention—on the absolute power of truly and authentically paying attention. I wanted to make attention matter.

I discovered that when we give what I call *intentional attention*, our attention pays. *Intention* is what makes *attention* valuable. Intentional attention pays in the form of:

- Deeper relationships at home and at work
- Productivity that actually drives results
- Improved client satisfaction and employee engagement
- Real, positive impact on the many issues our world currently faces
- A more meaningful, less stressful life

Intentional attention is a solution for our attention-deficit society as well as a proactive strategy for focusing on people, productivity, and our planet. And it is key to helping you get what you want in life.

INTENTIONAL ATTENTION

Listening with our eyes, as Donovan said, is one element of intentional attention. I think truly paying attention means listening with our eyes and our ears, thinking with our brains, understanding with our hearts, and giving with our souls. In more specific terms: *Intentional attention is conscious, deliberate, and transformational.* Let's take a look at each of these.

Conscious Versus Unconscious

When we think of someone lying in a hospital bed unconscious, that person isn't aware of or participating in what is going on around him or her. It's the same with attention. In our attention-deficit society, often the problem is not that we aren't paying attention, it's that we are doing so unconsciously rather than consciously.

We tend to operate in a world of our own—preoccupied with ourselves and our issues. We are multitasking, halfway listening to conversations, answering emails in meetings, or working out without thinking about our health goals. We give ourselves away by the faraway look in our eye and the redundant questions we ask. That kind of attention doesn't pay; it costs!

When we consciously pay attention, we are fully alert and present. We make direct eye contact throughout a conversation. We select our words for responsiveness. We are more interested in people than devices and are keenly aware of our surroundings. My friend Christian describes it as, "focusing solely on the task at hand whether that is a conversation with someone or something work related." Kellan, a human resources leader, puts it this way, "Conscious attention is being focused, engaged, and receptive."

To be conscious with our attention is to choose to be present in the moment and focused on the person, priority, or project in front of us. It requires us to decide to quiet the noise around us and the noise in our own head, because we all know it can be Crazy Town up there. It is making the choice to stop what we are doing—no matter how busy we might be—and to thoughtfully consider how to respond to email, answer a question, or provide a strategic response.

Deliberate Versus Distracted

In an attention-deficit society where too many of us are overworked, overstressed and overtired, we are often distracted by what is urgent rather than what is important. We are busy—always busy—but not productive. We are with people, but not the people who count. We work for hours, but are we getting any closer to achieving our goals?

Deliberate attention takes conscious choice to the next level with purpose and action. It means identifying the people, priorities, and passions that matter most in our lives and then purposefully and proactively focusing our conscious attention on them.

Conscious attention is stopping what we are doing on the computer to give our full focus to a team member who comes into our office to talk. Deliberate attention is purposely seeking out and recognizing a team member to thank them for the extra effort they put into the project. With conscious attention, we make a choice to put our phone on silent and then put it away during meals with others. Deliberate attention calls us to proactively set a dinner date with our significant other instead of just giving that person whatever we have left in the tank at the end of the day.

When I think of deliberate attention, I'm reminded of the military. In the military, the word *attention* is used in drill training, as in "come to attention." It's a way of marshalling people's focus and getting them prepared to take action on the next order. Attention in the military is a complete concentration of energy toward a specific purpose.

Deliberate attention is organizing your attention toward a particular purpose. It's saying *no* to some things so you can say *yes* to the important things that deserve your time and focus. It is scheduling time on your calendar to make progress on your goals rather than allowing your day to be consumed by interruptions, emails, and meetings.

Transformational Versus Transactional

When I started my career in banking, we talked about "transactions" when referring to customers. It was all about getting through one transaction just to get to the next one, instead of focusing on our customers and their needs. That bothered me. So, I made a point of always using names in our conversations, smiling at everyone (regardless of how grumpy they were), offering them a mint (especially if they had bad breath), and offering additional bank products and services (at the time I didn't know this was called add-on selling).

Those were the roots of what is now my personal philosophy: I want people to feel better because they interacted with me. I want to make sure they know that I see them, I hear them, and that they are the most important person to me in that moment.

When we are overworked, overstressed, and overtired, it's easy to go through life looking at our relationships, our work, and our daily activities as a series of transactions. That's often what we feel we have to do just to make it through the day. What if, instead of going through the motions, we invested our attention, our time, our efforts, and our caring in the people, priorities, and passions that are important to us? Could we make a difference? Absolutely! Not just an impact, but a transformational impact.

Instead of "doing business" with our attention, let's make a difference with our attention. Are you ever distracted in meetings, thinking about other work problems, counting the minutes until you can leave and get back to work? Instead of seeing it as "another meeting to sit through," what if you invested your attention in that meeting? What if you prepared for the meeting and reached out to the meeting facilitator to ask how you could support them? What if you were fully engaged in the meeting and added value by contributing? How might that impact the outcome? Now, imagine if everyone on *your* team invested the same level of attention in *your* meetings? Imagine the impact you would have at work and on people personally!

Transformational attention means holding our own agenda at bay and being outward rather than inward focused. It's being tuned in to the implications of our words, actions, and behaviors. It's listening to *listen*, instead of listening to respond. We can consciously choose to invest rather than waste our attention on a regular basis no matter how busy we perceive we are.

We have so many opportunities to make an impact through each interaction we have. When we give transformational attention, we can change a situation for the better, have a lasting effect on others, and drive results for the organization.

The Intentional Attention Model

To give intentional attention, we must choose consciously, act deliberately, and invest transformationally. One of my

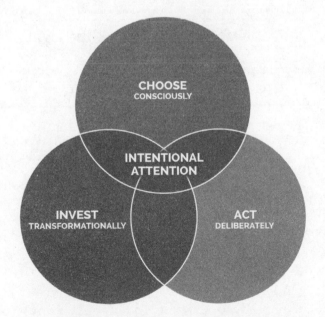

Figure 2.1. Intentional Attention

clients, Lina, had a great insight about intentional attention: "It means to bring your whole self to the situation. To be fully in the moment, and make the moment count." I couldn't agree more.

I am a huge fan of contextual models because they appeal to both the left and right hemispheres of our brain. Let's use one to capture what we know about intentional attention.

When you are in doubt about how to give your attention, use the following phrases (also shown in Figure 2.1), as your guide to give intentional attention:

- *Choose consciously—be in the moment*
- *Act deliberately—focus on what is important*
- *Invest transformationally—make an impact*

Intentional Attention—Shine the Light

I want to shine the light on attention as part of the Attention Revolution. I mean that figuratively and literally. Think of attention like a light source. Just as there are different types of light sources, there are different types of attention and each can be powerful and illuminating when used in the right situation. You can choose your attention depending on who is with you, what needs to be done, and how you want to achieve it.

Strobe Light Attention—A strobe (stroboscopic) light produces flashes of light. Stroboscopic originates from the Greek word *strobos* meaning "acts of whirling" or frenetic activity. This is the kind of unproductive frenetic attention we use when

---

we manic-task or check social media app after social media app while on a family outing. Strobe light attention is an advantage in a brainstorming meeting when you want a group of people to generate as many ideas as possible. The energy is high and ideas flow. Conversations move quickly and all ideas are considered.

Flashlight Attention—The light from a flashlight guides us, illuminates our way, and helps us search for important things. Flashlight attention will guide you down the right path when you consistently follow effective and proven processes, checklists, routines, and rituals. It is also the kind of attention you want as a leader, guiding the way for your team. Flashlight attention is damaging when you blindly follow someone's advice or a new process without questioning whether it will produce the return on your time and attention you require.

Spotlight Attention—A spotlight focuses a narrow, intense light beam. Likewise, spotlight attention helps you narrow your focus and intensify your productivity. It is exceptional when you're in a conversation with someone you value or on a tight deadline and you need to block out the distractions of the world around you. This type of focused attention has damaging results when you hyperfocus only on the negative aspects of yourself or others.

Which light do you need for the task at hand? Ask that first and you will be well on your way to being deliberate in your attention.

How do we put this model into practice and give intentional attention every day so that our attention pays? Glad you asked! We are going to have to give up some of our bad habits. We are going to have to move beyond unconscious attention to conscious attention, from distracted to deliberate, and make a shift from transactional to transformational.

In short, we're going to have to do the dreaded C *word*—CHANGE!

CHANGE IS HARD—BUT OH SO WORTH IT!

John (minor details changed to protect his identity) was a senior executive in the investment banking industry. His high-profile role required his creative input to multiple projects, while building a significant team to help change the industry. His revolutionary ideas were inspiring and his energy level was always high (almost intense). But his email inbox was constantly full, his phone constantly ringing, and meeting invitations never ending. He would literally run from one meeting to the next and had developed a reputation for often being late.

From the moment he opened his eyes in the wee hours of the morning, until the moment he closed his eyes (often in the wee hours of the morning), he was constantly connected to his team, his phone, and his clients. Regardless of what time he started or what time he finished each workday, he could never get it all done. He sent requests to his team at all hours of the day and night (and they would respond). He developed a reputation for his late-night requests.

His family suffered. His health, and especially his sleep, suffered. His performance was high, but leadership feared one of their highest performing executives would not just burn out but flame out. I was hired to work with him to explore how he could change his brain, change his focus, and change his habits to achieve his objectives and create more work-life integration.

After much convincing, we created a radical plan for change. He identified who and what was most important to him. We made him take a vacation with his family (with full leadership support) to a remote island where no one could contact him. We also encouraged him to find some new hobbies. We made changes to his calendar and helped him stop some bad habits like emailing the team after hours. I coached him how to say *no* to some things so he could say *yes* to the things that mattered.

As a result of these changes, his team was happier and even thanked me for getting their evening hours back. His family was delighted to have time with him, and he was healthier and less stressed. And the business portfolio grew significantly. John discovered that intentional attention does, in fact, pay!

Our attention-deficit society has caused many of us to lose our focus and develop some bad attention habits, just like John did. We've given up control over attention. It's time to take it back. And you know what that means—we're going to have to make some changes. If we want to be intentional with our attention, we need to change our brains, change our focus, and change our habits.

Change Your Brain

Have you heard the assertion that the human attention span has decreased to the point that we now have the attention span of a goldfish?

Good news—it's not true! Not only is it not true; it's absolutely ridiculous! Who on earth wants their attention span measured in terms of a goldfish? Not me, no thank you!

This is a marketing myth that was repeated by bloggers and authors and went viral. It's not based on any validated research that I've been able to find and yet, it is constantly requoted. Even without scientific evidence to the contrary, we know it's not true. If we had the attention span of a goldfish, no one would ever binge-watch their favorite TV shows.

Every human brain has the ability to lend its attentive capacity to a particular task for a particular amount of time. When the time expires, we can choose the same task as the next subject of sustained attention. In other words, we have the ability to pay attention to what we want to pay attention to (as evidenced by our binge-watching and social media obsessions).

Our attention span is not decreasing. We are allowing it to be split among multiple stimuli, inputs, devices, and media. If we want our attention to pay, the first change we need to make is to retrain our brain to ignore distractions and interruptions.

Scientific models of attention refer to *bottleneck* models. Our brains receive an incredible volume of sensory inputs, so much that the brain cannot consciously process all of it. This limited processing capacity creates a bottleneck, so to speak. Only some information gets through the bottleneck.

It makes sense that when our brains are overloaded by too much stimuli and information, we are easily distracted. If we can simplify and reduce the stimuli (less information trying to get through the bottleneck), we improve our focus. Think of an all-white room with just one red object. What would you focus on? You would likely be drawn to the one red object because all the other stimuli are gone. When we limit our inputs, we maximize our attention. One way to do this is to minimize distractions and interruptions by taking control of our devices, apps, and social media. We'll discuss this in greater detail in later chapters.

Another way to maximize our attention is to help our brain filter what is important. Did you know your brain has a *reticular activation system*? I call it RAZ for short. (Yes, it should be RAS, but this little Aussie does things a little differently!)

The RAZ filters incoming information and stimuli and determines what you pay attention to. How does it know what to let through and what to filter out? The RAZ works to make you right. Whatever you think or believe about a situation, your RAZ will set out to find examples that support your belief. Your RAZ also filters out extraneous information so you can focus on information that is connected to situations that are important to you. If you are a parent, you know that you can pick your child's voice or cry out of a room full of noisy children. That is your RAZ at work.

Think of your RAZ as radar constantly searching for information related to those things that are important to you or that supports your thinking about a situation. Think about the last time you bought a new car. What type, brand, model, and color did you buy? After you bought your new car, did you start to notice all the cars just like yours on the road? Those cars were always there; you simply hadn't noticed them. Your RAZ had filtered them out because they weren't important to you before.

You can leverage your RAZ to help you pay attention. When you identify what is important to you, your brain will naturally help you pay more attention to it. I call this *revving your RAZ*. Let's find out how to do that.

Change Your Focus

Your brain is an attention machine. It's going to pay attention to *something*. The question is *what*? Are you going to allow it to pay attention to things that are irrelevant to your goals, dreams, and desires (that is, Facebook, news, and so on)?

Or are you going to choose to pay attention to the people, priorities, and passions that are important in your life? Who is in control—you or your brain?

When we make something important, our RAZ and brain will give it attention. If we perceive someone (or something) as not important it doesn't get (or deserve) our attention. How do we elevate the importance of someone (or something) to make it worthy of our attention? By proactively and deliberately identifying the people, priorities, and passions that we care about.

Too often, we go through life dealing with the urgent rather than the important. But life has a funny way of getting our attention, often when we least expect it. Have you noticed that when our health is challenged, we suddenly realize our health matters? For some it's an event that triggers reflection on who and what really matters. Maybe you hear someone you knew died, and you wish you could turn back time and have one last conversation with them. Or you start to think about where you are in life and what you still want to accomplish. Or perhaps you narrowly avoid a car accident and you realize what could have happened to you and your family. Suddenly your family becomes incredibly dear to you and you savor every moment with them.

Is that really how you want to go through life? Discovering what is important only *after* a jarring wake-up call? Why not let this be your wake-up call instead? Why not make a commitment right now, today, to clearly identify who and what truly matters to you?

Stop trying to be all things to all people. Stop trying to do everything. Stop trying to be everywhere and part of every conversation.

Start focusing on developing deeper relationships. Start focusing on completing the highest priority projects. Start focusing on strategic opportunities that give you the highest return on your investment of attention.

Only you can determine who and what matters in your life. There is no magic prescription, no magic formula or a get-rich-quick-get-skinny-overnight type of template you can buy on the home shopping network. Everyone has an opinion; only you can say what matters to you. Stop right now and answer these questions:

Who matters most to you in your life?

What projects and opportunities are your highest priorities?

What passions do you most want to pursue?

Identifying what matters to you will rev up your RAZ. Just shifting your focus to these people, priorities, and passions will help you give intentional attention to them. As a result, you will strengthen your relationships with people at work and home, achieve quicker completion on projects and consensus in meetings at work, and contribute more effectively in community events and conversations.

Change Your Habits

In our attention-deficit society, it feels like we are moving faster than ever before. We think we have to be constantly connected to our devices, email, and social media. It's simply not true. These are just bad habits we have allowed ourselves to form. We need to break some of these habits and replace them with new, positive habits that focus our attention on what matters most.

To stop a bad habit, we need to understand what triggers that habit. Psychologists have developed a schematic called a *habit loop*, which consists of three parts. The first part of the loop is known as the *cue*. This is the trigger that causes the brain to initiate the automatic behavior. Technology is a major attention trigger. For example, consider the habit of checking your phone. The cue or trigger is the noise or vibration alert that signals you have a new email, text, or social media update. Even if your phone is in your pocket and on silent mode, the moment you feel it vibrate, your brain is triggered and your attention is immediately split.

Following the cue is the behavior itself, called the *routine*. In our example, the routine would be reaching for your phone. The final part of the habit loop is the *reward*, which in our case is seeing who just texted you or finding out what is trending on social media.

Understanding this habit loop is critical to breaking our negative attention habits. We need to know the negative attention triggers that are damaging to our relationships and productivity and to achieving our goals. Then we need to take responsibility for changing our behavior by eliminating those triggers. Instead of putting your phone in your pocket or on the table where you can still see and hear it, silence it and put it in a drawer, briefcase, or purse. Better yet—turn it off completely when you're with someone, in a meeting or working on a task.

Finally, repeat the new behavior until it becomes a habit. Have you heard the tired, overused phrase, *It takes 21 days to create a new habit*? It's not true! It's frustratingly been quoted by many a trainer and motivational speaker (including me before I realized the error of my ways).

A study conducted by Phillippa Lally, a health psychology researcher at University College London, aimed to figure out just how long it actually takes to form a habit. Their findings, published in the *European Journal of Social Psychology*, showed that it takes more than two months on average before a new behavior becomes automatic—66 days, to be exact. (The study also found that "missing one opportunity to perform the behavior did not materially affect the habit formation process." Meaning, it doesn't matter if you mess up every now and then. Creating a new habit is not an all-or-nothing process.

The negative attention habits we have created with technology, social media, and a lack of business etiquette can be changed. Yes, it will take more than 21 days, but it will be well worth it. When we stop the habits that are getting in the way of us being intentional with our attention, our attention will pay big dividends both personally and professionally.

What habits do you need to break when it comes to how you are choosing to invest your attention?

We asked clients and colleagues what bad attention behaviors drive them crazy. The list was very long—too long to include here. Following are just a few of the most common bad habits and how you can replace them with an intentional attention habit.

Bad Attention Habit	Intentional Attention Habit
Constantly checking cell phones in meetings.	Leave it at your desk, in a bag, switch to silent, or turn it over and avoid being distracted.
Arriving late to meetings, asking redundant questions, being unprepared, having sidebar conversations, or going off on tangents.	Arrive on time. Listen intently. Take notes. Stay focused. Stick to the agenda. Be quiet.
Looking behind or around the person you are speaking with for someone more important to talk with.	Give undivided attention to the person in front of you in every conversation.

(continued)

Bad Attention Habit	Intentional Attention Habit
Asking, "How are you?" or "How was your weekend?" and then keep walking.	Ask, stop, and listen.
Responding to texts, emails, and voicemail messages when with another person.	Put your devices away. Be present. If you need to have it close by, explain that to the other person and then excuse yourself and answer privately.
Looking at your device, answering emails on your computer, or wearing headphones when someone is talking with you.	Close your screen, remove headphones, listen, and respond. Step away from the keyboard.
Finishing people's sentences, interrupting conversations, or asking the same question continuously.	Listen to listen, then respond, or just be quiet.
Blocking the aisle with a shopping cart or not returning it to the designated areas.	Be a good human, consider others, don't be lazy.
Photographing or videoing every aspect of the event or meal.	Enjoy the moment, capture a memory, then put devices away.
Spelling or pronouncing someone's name incorrectly.	Be diligent with names; it's one of the most important ways to pay attention.
Using fidget spinners.	Stop it. Be a grown up.
Ignoring texts, emails, or voicemail messages.	Use out of office or voicemail to manage expectations.

Bad Attention Habit	Intentional Attention Habit
Walking on the wrong side of the walkway, looking down at your cell phone while walking in the streets and bumping into people.	Look up. People aren't responsible for your safety.
Answering the phone saying, "Sorry, I cannot talk now."	Let it go to voicemail.
When traveling, not having identification and boarding pass ready when you get to the front of the line, wearing anything that sets off security, or removing the wrong bag at baggage claim.	Be prepared with documents, smile at the TSA agent, remove potential items for security, consider a travel uniform for a speedy process, and mark your bag with something unique.

Philosopher and motivational speaker Jim Rohn is quoted as saying, "Motivation is what gets you started. Habit is what keeps you going." If you took the time to answer the questions in the previous section, you have discovered your motivation for change—the people, priorities, and passions that are most important to you. Now, keep it going by developing some new habits that will help you consistently give intentional attention to the things that matter most.

HOW TO MAKE YOUR ATTENTION PAY

As leaders, we have one life to lead, on this one planet, and yet we juggle a multitude of roles at work, at home, and in our communities. To help us focus our attention and not split this precious resource, we need to create a simple structure

Figure 2.2. Attention Pays Framework

for how to give intentional attention in all aspects of our life. I call this the *Attention Pays Framework* and it looks like this:

Personally—Be Thoughtful with *who* gets your attention. Intentional attention starts with you. To assist and serve others, you have to focus on you first. You have to be the most confident, successful person you can be. Then you can focus on the VIPs—very important people—in your life, both personally and professionally, who also need your attention.

Professionally—Be Productive as an individual and leader and take action on *what* is the most important use of your attention. Again, we focus on you first so you can achieve your professional objectives. Only then can you help your team overcome their attention challenges and achieve better results.

Globally—Be Responsible for *how* you contribute to your local community and your world. Find something you believe in and then give intentional attention to that passion to create a bigger impact.

This framework takes everything we have talked about with respect to intentional attention and shows you how to apply it to your everyday life. The rest of this book addresses the elements of the Attention Pays Framework. Each chapter will give you practical strategies to help you choose consciously, act deliberately, and invest your attention transformationally. (If you are a business owner or leader of influence in your organization and want to know how your company can give intentional attention, make sure you read the Bonus Chapter, "Build an Organization that Pays Attention.")

Some of the strategies in the coming chapters may seem obvious, simple, or maybe even common sense. They are. This is not rocket science (no offense to my clients who are actual rocket scientists!). However, just because they are common sense doesn't mean they are common practice. In fact, companies consistently hire me to help their top leaders implement these very same strategies. Why? Because so few leaders are doing them—and because they work!

Most of us just need a (not so gentle) reminder every now and then to do the things we often already know we should be doing. As you go through these chapters, make a note of where you can take action and make a greater impact on your attention. If you will implement even a few of the strategies, you will change your brain, change your focus, and change your habits. Before you know it, you will see the return on your attention investment at work, at home, and in your community.

The place to start is with you.

Today, I challenge you to invest one minute, in one interaction, to create one significant moment, for just one person that may create one memory that will last a lifetime.

Make Your Attention Pay

1. Where can you listen with your eyes more?

2. What distractions can you eliminate to be more deliberate with your attention?

3. Where can you take action to be more transformational than transactional with your attention?

4. What bad habits do you need to replace with good intentional attention habits?

PART TWO

Personally—Be Thoughtful

CHAPTER 3

Personalize Performance: Brand Building, Nido Qubein Style

One of the best role models of intentional attention I know is president of High Point University, Dr. Nido Qubein. I've observed him as a speaker, philanthropist, and we've served together on a national industry board. When you meet Dr. Qubein, he is impeccably dressed, eloquent, and elegant in every environment, a continuous learner, positioning himself to learn from the best, and generously sharing what he learns.

He is an accomplished businessman, generous donor, board member of multiple companies, talented speaker, and prolific author. He constantly impresses with professional achievements, personal drive, commitment, and demonstrated integrity.

His day begins at 4 a.m. He focuses on giving first, writing at least four notes of appreciation daily, constantly studying business and world leaders, inviting them to be interviewed at High Point to share thinking and success stories with students. He is committed to his students, their families, the community, and our environment.

He is grooming future leaders, creating extraordinary experiences for students and impacting the city of High Point, North Carolina, with development of infrastructure on campus and surrounding areas. One of his most impressive skills I noticed while in his company is that every student who approached him, he knew their name! He's not even their teacher; he's the president of the whole university.

Dr. Qubein epitomizes the first element of the Attention Pays Framework: personally—be thoughtful. He gives conscious, deliberate, and transformational attention daily not only to himself but also to others. Influential leaders like Dr. Qubein know they must be kind to and communicate thoughtfully with their family, friends, team, boss, within their organization, and most importantly with themselves.

Too often today, in our busy overwhelmed state, we are not paying attention and that is often viewed as being thoughtless. We don't use people's names, we forget our manners (please and thank you are vital), and we don't remember special occasions for people we love (and need Facebook to remind us one of our family members is having a birthday). We are just as thoughtless with ourselves. We take our health for granted. We don't offer ourselves the kindness and attention we deserve.

Being thoughtful is the opposite of thoughtless. One of the mantras of the Attention Revolution is to be thought-*full* not thoughtless. This means slowing down and taking time to give intentional attention to the people who matter most to us. I am a big believer in systemized thoughtfulness, meaning we need to make time for kindness by creating routines. This chapter and Chapter 4 are all about creating systems to give intentional attention to ourselves and to others.

This chapter is all about being thoughtful to yourself. It's all about you. That's not being selfish or self-absorbed. It's about self-care, and being self-full. Every time you fly, you hear the flight attendant say to put on your oxygen mask before assisting others. That's because you can't help those around you if you're passed out cold. The same is true with your personal attention. You have to first take care of yourself. When you are healthy, happy, and calm, you can then assist and serve others. Being thoughtful with yourself is paying attention to your health, your energy and stress levels, your spirituality (whatever that means to you), and your relationships.

Chapter 4 is about being thoughtful toward others. It is an outward focus of your personal attention. It's about giving intentional attention to the people who are most important in your life, personally and professionally. Being thoughtful is considering other's needs and being in tune with their feelings and conversations. Your attention is one of the greatest gifts you can give others, but first you must focus on how to take care of yourself, your communication skills, and your personal brand.

PRACTICE SELF-CARE

I love this quote from Parker Palmer, author of *Let Your Life Speak*, who says, "Self-care is never a selfish act—it is simply good stewardship of the only gift I have, the gift I was put on earth to offer others. Anytime we can listen to true self and give the care it requires, we do it not only for ourselves, but for the many others whose lives we touch."

When you give yourself the attention you deserve, it will return tenfold. Let's look at some strategies for taking care of you.

Establish a Morning Routine

Making an impact at home, work, and in your community starts with your physical, mental, and spiritual well-being. Consider establishing an effective morning routine to pay attention to how you begin each day and set the tone for what you will achieve to create habits of attentiveness.

- *Meditate*—Before you think I am asking you to sit on the floor cross-legged chanting *ommmmm*, consider that meditation takes many forms: walking in nature, listening to music, inspirational reading, writing in a journal, or the act of meditating. Admittedly, I have struggled with this and find meditation apps on my phone help enormously. Successful business leaders, actors, and musicians practice mediation daily and attribute this ritual to their success, including Oprah, the late Steve Jobs, Jennifer Aniston, Clint Eastwood, and Madonna.

> Go to neenjames.com/extras for my favorite Attention Resources, including my favorite meditation apps.

- *Exercise*—Working out strengthens physical and mental abilities, assists in balancing your brain chemically, and allows you to approach each day with energy. While I don't know the secret to falling in love with exercise, I do understand it is vital to our health, and that's a good enough reason for me. To keep your interest in moving your body, consider varying your exercise. I love Barre3, Peloton, running, lifting weights, yoga, and even heading out for a walk. Don't make it complicated, but do make it part of your everyday routine to take care of the one body you are given.

- *Eat*—Preparing a healthy breakfast gives your brain and body the nutrients needed to manage the challenges of your day ahead. When you skip breakfast you tell yourself you are not important enough to take just a few minutes to give your body the fuel it requires to get through the day. Make this really simple and find ways to streamline your morning routine. I have found there are services that can deliver pre-chopped, in containers, super-healthy smoothies that I pop in the freezer. When I'm ready to have one, I just add water (or coconut water if I am feeling extra special), blend for a moment, and I am out the door! In winter, I love oats mixed with a little brown sugar or maple syrup because it is warm and cozy. I can't provide nutritional advice but I can tell you that your brain needs nutrients to help you function, pay attention, and make decisions in your day. Don't skip breakfast. Period.

- Now you are ready to start the day!

Establish a Night Routine

In our book *Folding Time*, we shared the importance of a night routine. We call it sleep hygiene, and no, it's not just clean sheets! Sleep hygiene is a series of habits to allow you to create an environment for your best night's sleep.

Growing research and health experts are sharing the importance of sleep and the impact on our health and ability to achieve results. Many executives pride themselves on only needing a few hours' sleep. I think they are misguided. Think of your body as a Ferrari—a sexy, red sports car that needs fuel and maintenance to perform at the highest level. Just like a Ferrari needs pit stops and fuel to function, so does your body. Sleep is not negotiable; it's vital.

Sleep hygiene is another form of self-care. Try these strategies:

- *Create the ideal sleep environment*—comfortable bed, your favorite pillow, proper room temperature, blackout lining or dark curtains (to block out light), and a room that is relaxing and pleasant.

- *Prepare for sleep*—create a getting ready for bed routine that requires you to do the same thing each night (regardless of where you are in the world) so that you send signals to your body that it is time for sleep.

- *Avoid stimulants*—caffeine, nicotine, and alcohol too close to bedtime disrupts your sleep patterns.

- *Avoid heavy meals*—some foods require more energy to process so consider the timing of your meals and the foods you eat later in the night as they can affect your sleep.

- *Keep technology out of the bedroom*—your bedroom is for two things, sleeping and sex. Devices and television can interfere with both of those activities. The blue light emitted from cell phones restrains the production of melatonin, the hormone that controls your sleep–wake cycle or circadian rhythm. If you need an alarm clock, buy one.

- *Stop working in bed*—I am guilty of this, too! It's easy to grab for your phone first thing in the morning if you have it beside your bed and start scrolling through email and social media. Stop it! Associate your bed with pleasurable activities, not work-related tasks.

Paying attention to your health and your sleep are great ways to demonstrate self-care.

Schedule Recovery Time

We are great at scheduling meetings and appointments with others, but not so good at scheduling time for ourselves. To continue to operate at a high level you need recovery time. Athletes tell you their scheduled recovery time is as important as their training time. What vacations have you planned this year? Have you scheduled time for a short break, perhaps a long weekend? Don't be proud of the fact you haven't had a vacation in a long period of time.

Do you enjoy fishing, or spa treatments, or maybe getting lost in a great book? Schedule downtime, make appointments to give you something to look forward to in your busy week, and treat this appointment as an important part of your week.

Personalize Performance

Henry was an executive in a major hospital system. He worked long hours, volunteered at his daughter's school, served on a community advisory board, managed a large, high-profile team, was studying for his MBA, and traveled every week for work. His team members complained to the executive team that he never responded to their email requests and was always late for meetings. In addition, he regularly cancelled their one-on-one appointments, and when they did meet with him, he was often abrupt, dismissive, and aggressive. Leadership realized he was overwhelmed and hired me to work with him.

After several honest and very direct conversations, we determined he was trying to do it all with no success. He had to make some changes, and he did:

- He decided to defer his studies for one semester to focus on work commitments.

- He resigned from the advisory board so he could focus more time with his daughter's school.

- He delegated meeting attendance to other team members to raise their visibility in the company

- He scheduled monthly one-on-one meetings with team members offsite so they wouldn't be distracted by hospital busyness.

- He hired a personal trainer to get in shape and manage his stress levels.

When I checked in with his team 90 days later, they told me he was a completely different person. Actually, he was the same person; he'd just had a significant wake-up call. He realized if his family resented his work and his team resented his leadership, he wasn't contributing the way he wanted. He couldn't be all things to all people. He has since completed his MBA, lost weight, run a half marathon, and got promoted to a very senior role within his organization. Attention really does pay!

Set Boundaries with Your Devices and Social Media

I am not a technology or social media hater. I just think they have their place. Everything in moderation, as they say.

For your personal sanity and safety, it's time to change your relationship with your devices and social media:

- Unsubscribe to anything that doesn't positively feed your soul. I love the gif that says, "Please cancel my subscription to your issues." Decide what you will expose your mind to. Get off any lists or leave groups that are not a good investment of your attention or affect your emotions negatively.

- Place devices in your glove compartment before driving to avoid the temptation of checking messages or social media while behind the wheel.

- If you need to use your device for directions, consider mounting a device attachment so you don't have to touch it while driving and allow you to focus on the road.

- Stop texting and driving—just stop it. Remember, nine people die daily because of distracted driving.

- Create a password for your cell phone to protect your information. I use a number that is a financial goal; each time I enter the password I'm reminded to take action toward that number.

- Stop taking your cell phone to the bathroom; it's unhygienic and disgusting. Something that makes me crazy is when I can hear people having conversations in the airport bathroom stalls. I might be known to occasionally press extra flushes just to make more noise (I know that makes me a bad human).

- Leave your phone at home (I know that sounds crazy), when you are with people you care about, or at the gym completing a workout.

MANAGE YOUR PERSONAL BRAND

What Does Your Personal Brand Say About You?

Ryan (not his real name) was an executive in research with one of our clients. He was technically brilliant, well liked, and wicked smart but constantly overlooked for promotions. His company invited me to consult with him, explaining that he had no executive presence. His colleagues told me, "Ryan is so smart, but he's so disorganized, always late, and misses deadlines." Do you know someone like this in your organization?

Ryan needed an updated personal brand, instruction on how to have professional presence, and an internal public relations campaign. Together we created a 90-day accountability plan to fix his personal brand, improve his productivity, and correct negative feedback he was getting from leaders and peers. He worked with a stylist to update his work wardrobe, recruited the administrative assistant to create systems for paper flow, implemented email management strategies, and dissected his calendar. We reviewed Power-Point decks to streamline messages and created contextual models to help others understand key messages. We worked on body language, tone of voice, speaking up in meetings, and challenged him to start listening more intently instead of interrupting people.

His leaders told me the work we did together was transformational, sharing that they finally saw the diamond that was previously in the rough. He went on to be promoted within 110 days of us working together and has gone from strength to strength while raising a family and volunteering at a local homeless shelter.

Your personal brand is how others perceive you—your skills, executive presence, and the contributions you make. Jeff Bezos, CEO of Amazon says, "Your brand is what other people say about you when you are not in the room." It is crucial to your success in job interviews, applying for promotions, starting your own company, presenting at a conference or internal meeting, or serving in your local community.

What does your personal brand stand for? Do you know what other people say about you when you're not in the room?

Corporate brands spend billions of dollars each year managing perceptions of products in the marketplace. You are a product in your workplace and in your community. Investing intentional attention in creating a strong personal brand is vital if you want to attract the right type of attention in your personal and professional life. Enhance your personal brand with these strategies:

- *Conduct a brand audit*—If you are unsure about your personal brand, ask five people you trust to describe you in three words. Notice the similarities and characteristics they share that indicate how you are perceived.

- *Create brand guidelines*—Establish personal rules for yourself and be consistent.

- *Choose your wardrobe carefully*—Every outfit you wear signals to the world how you want to be treated.

- *Invest in quality accessories*—Your pen, bag, wallet, luggage, and glasses are all reflections of your style and reflect how you pay attention to details.

- *Surround yourself*—with people with whom you are proud to be associated.

- *Be generous*—with your time and resources.

- *Strategically use social media platforms*—Our policy is to never post anything negative and we don't allow pictures to be tagged or posted online without approval.

- *Be consistent*—in your dress, speech, action, and communication.

- *Update your voicemail*—allow callers to experience your personality with an interesting message.

- *Change your email signature*—Include relevant contact information and a quote or website for more information about you and your company.

- *Send interesting* out of office *messages*—Grab your email readers' attention with clever messages that surprise them.

- *Be attentive in meetings and videoconferences*—Be engaged; don't check email or text messages.

- *Walk into the room with purpose*—Have your phone put away before you enter the room; smile, shake hands, and acknowledge people around you.

- *Be well read*—Subscribe to magazines, read blogs, listen to podcasts, and review executive book summaries. This allows you to have an interesting conversation with anyone you meet.

- *Always have a question*—In a company town hall style meeting or at a conference, ask a strategic question of the speaker or leader that will benefit everyone in the room.

- *Establish a personal development plan*—Include a daily reading file, watch TED talks, read blogs, attend training programs, and listen to podcasts.

- *Develop strong presentation skills*—for internal meetings, company updates, and any time you present ideas to a group of people.

- *Invest in mentors and coaches*—to accelerate development areas of productivity, presentation, and leadership skills.

- *Attend industry conferences and networking events*—Prepare an interesting response to the question, "So what do you do?"

Become Your Own Publicist

The role of a publicist is to share good news, achievements, and upcoming events. Celebrities have them and organizations hire them. Do you need one? Absolutely! Some people assume if they do a good job, they will be noticed. Wrong. Many leaders are busy and distracted and they don't always notice the accomplishments of you and your team. To stay *top of mind* with leadership, become your own publicist and consider an internal public relations campaign:

- Email five bullet points to your boss every Friday outlining the accomplishments of you and your team for the week as an informal status report.

- Seek out opportunities to share resources with internal newsletters, such as industry and company publications in your community.

- Volunteer to provide updates, share presentations, or serve on panel discussions, at team meetings, and in industry conferences.

- Offer to lead team meetings, town hall events, or co-chair an internal conference.

- Interview key leaders on their success and then send their notes to them to share with others.

Always Plan for the Next Opportunity

Leaders with a strong personal brand know where they are going next. They are always keeping an eye out for the next promotion or opportunity for development. Following are my two favorite strategies if you want to make a strong impression, stand out in a job interview, get noticed among your colleagues, or be considered for a promotion into a new role at work:

1. *Create a picture of your First 100 Days.* Former President Franklin D. Roosevelt created the idea of the 100-day plan in his radio address on July 24, 1933. Every president is now assessed on what they accomplish in their first 100 days in office. Create a plan that outlines what you would hope to achieve in a new role in the first 100 days on the job or on the team. I have coached several executives to use this strategy when seeking a promotion at work or shifting companies, and this was the piece that set them apart in the interview.

2. *Develop a 90-day performance promotional strategy.* Early in my banking career, I noticed that people who get things done get promoted. I challenged myself to create a 90-day promotional strategy. I determined it would take me 90 days to learn a new job, the next 90 days to master it, and then another 90 days to identify and train a successor. I figured within 12 months, I could be promoted. That means I was hyper-focused on significantly upping my performance every 90 days. It might sound crazy (and ambitious), but if you track my banking career, I was promoted, on average, every 10 months. Can you develop an accelerated promotion strategy for yourself and your team members to ensure you remain constantly focused on growth and development? Ninety days is a great amount of time to see a change in results, a shift in behaviors, and the rewards of focused activity.

Find and Connect with Advocates

Advocates are people inside or outside your organization who believe in your abilities and are willing to recommend, refer, and promote you. They are vital to your career. These important relationships require you to invest time, attention, and energy diligently.

Seek out people who like what you are doing and will share their experience of you with others. Have you ever had some of your customers, clients, or team members love what you do so much that they refer you to others? They are your advocates. Think of your advocates as a secret sales force, out there promoting you to their network. If you have your own company you might consider people who will actively advocate for you and your business and recommend you to others.

Create a list of your top 20 most important advocates and schedule a *connection point* with each one every six to eight weeks to give them intentional attention. Here are some ways to let your advocates know you are thinking of them:

- Leave a voicemail of appreciation.
- Forward a blog or share a podcast.
- Send a handwritten note.
- Text a photo of an experience you enjoyed together.
- Post an encouraging or fun comment on social media profiles.
- Send a gift such as a book, magazine subscription, movie or theater tickets, or their favorite brand of coffee, tea, or alcohol.
- Invite them as your guest to a networking or fundraising event.

Who could you approach to advocate for you this week?

Be the Duck

Have you ever watched a duck at the pond glide effortlessly across the water and then jump out and shake off their feathers? What you can't see underneath are the little legs paddling like crazy! As leaders, we need to be like a duck to manage how we are perceived. Here's how:

- *Remain calm*—regardless of big goals or stressful meetings. Keep your cool.

- *Stay focused*—Don't get upset or flustered, look elegant and in control and remain focused on the achievement of your goals.

- *Shake off negativity*—Avoid conversations, gossip, or thought patterns that distract you.

Seek Feedback

Are you surrounded by people eager to give feedback? We live in a society where people feel it is their right to share opinions and unsolicited feedback with you in person, at meeting and events, and online through email and social media. I disagree that everyone is qualified to give it to you. My rule: I am incredibly selective of who is allowed to speak into my life. They must be qualified and have permission to give it. Unsolicited negative feedback and comments can distract you and affect your performance. Here are some strategies for handling feedback:

- *Consider the source*—Determine who is qualified to give you feedback based on their relationships and expertise.

- *Hire professionals*—When seeking qualified expertise, you may benefit from investing in a professional coach, mentor, personal trainer, nutritionist, or stylist.

- *Ignore trolls*—You may encounter negative people on social media and blogs (and in real life), and it's best to not give them any of your time and attention. Set policy and safeguards for you personally to laugh off the craziness, and use your principles as your guide. Don't respond.

- *Avoid drama*—Don't participate on social media platforms or discussion groups where you will be exposed to negative sources that won't provide valuable feedback.

- *Set up the environment*—Determine the best way to receive the feedback. Is it face-to-face, over the phone, in an email, or by videoconference?

MANAGE YOUR COMMUNICATIONS
Grow Your Confidence

Do you know someone who exudes confidence when they walk into a room? They have presence—their outfit, posture, and style all send the message that they are poised and self-assured. They present their ideas with authority, certainty, and knowledge.

How confident are you? Do you think others see you the same way you see yourself? Confidence gets positive attention and is a skill that can be developed. Here are some strategies to help you do that:

- *Know yourself*—Invest time in learning your strengths and stressors by reading books such as *Fascinate* by Sally Hogshead and *Strengths Finder 2.0* by Tom Rath, and by completing online assessment tools like DiSC, Myers-Briggs, Insights, or Highland Ability Battery. How can you leverage your strengths this week?

- *Articulate three things you are good at*—Early in my career, one of my best (and hardest) bosses, Barbara, gave me powerful advice as a young manager, advice that has served my entire corporate and entrepreneurial career, saying, "Neen, you need to articulate three things you are good at, don't blink and don't look away." The simplicity of this advice worked in every job interview, promotional opportunity, and new client appointments. What are your three?

- *Believe in your ideas*—Do you present your ideas with conviction and make them easily understood to those in meetings and presentations? What do you stand for?

- *Position your unique thoughts*—Your ability to present your ideas as contextual visual models and concise statements will help you stand out in the room (more on contextual models in Chapter 5). How can you capture your thoughts visually?

Be Conscious of Your Language

Due to our distracted and often split attention, we aren't always purposeful in how we choose our words and actions. Do the words you use provide positive or negative attention? My motivational speaker friend and author of *Doing What Must Be Done,* Chad Hymas, often challenges audiences, "Where can you replace the words *I, me, my* with *you, we,* and *ours?*" This is great advice for inclusive and collaborative language.

Remove overused, cliché phrases and replace them with words that help build a stronger personal brand. See the following chart for some of my least favorite words and some suggested replacements. Listen to how often you use these words and consider changing them.

Remove from Your Language	Replace With
But or *however*	Simply make your point and stop talking; replace with *and*.
Problem or *issue*	*Challenge* or *opportunity* (which implies a solution)
Should	*Would you consider?*
They work for me.	*They work with me.*
My team	*Our team*
Take it to the next level	*Accelerate results, create progress*, or *improve performance*
Push the envelope	*Explore boundaries* or *overcome objections*
Outside the box	*creative, innovative, ground breaking*

Every year for the past 10 years, I present intentional attention strategies in the Comcast Center in Philadelphia to the incredible young leaders at City Year, sponsored by the leadership team at Comcast. City Year Philadelphia deploys over 200 highly skilled AmeriCorps members to serve in 14 schools. Together, this team positively impacts the students in the city at public and charter schools.

Over the years, I have stayed in contact with many of these leaders. They tell me that paying attention to their personal brand, their communication, and their relationships has helped them achieve greater success in all aspects of their lives. They also say that they shared these strategies in their schools, workplaces, and homes. I am so proud of these leaders and the huge impact they make in the world. Their selfless leadership impacts the lives of future generations.

Leave a legacy as a leader who is focused, deliberate, and influential. Be a role model. Be a leader of integrity who does what they say they will do.

Make Your Attention Pay

1. What new morning and night routines can you create to practice self-care?

2. Which boundaries will you implement to better manage your devices and social media?

3. What actions will you take to enhance your personal brand this week?

4. Which words will you stop using this week?

CHAPTER 4

Focus on VIPs: Systemize Thoughtfulness

Whatever we put our attention on will grow stronger.
—Maharishi Mahesh Yogi

With all respect to Maharishi Mahesh Yogi, I would add one minor upgrade to this wisdom: "Whatever—or *whomever*—we put our attention on will grow stronger."

Wanting and needing attention is a basic human need. It's how our brains are wired. As I said earlier, every person wants to feel that they are the center of somebody's attention, even if they don't want to be the center of everybody's attention.

Who in your life is getting your attention? And what kind of attention are they getting?

Your way of thinking, your attitudes, and your opinions affect how you determine with whom to invest your attention. We need to consider the people we want to be surrounded with, who we care for, and who deserve our attention. We also need to understand how we can give intentional attention to these very important people.

FOCUS ON YOUR VIPS

Who Needs Your Attention in Your Personal Life?

When speaking with audiences, I often ask, "What matters most to you?" Far and away, the most common response is always, "Family."

The concept of *family* has different meanings, which can extend beyond blood relations. As a happy little Aussie (also a U.S. citizen), my American friends are the family I have chosen. (That doesn't make my Aussie family any less important.) For many of us, family might include neighbors, friends, and furry friends. Some people even enjoy their friends more than their family!

No matter how you describe the very important people (VIPs) in your life, are they getting the best of you? Are you giving them your intentional attention every day? Does your family get your undivided attention when you enter your home? Or are they getting the leftovers of your day—whatever time, energy, and attention might be left over after your work obligations are met?

We are often paid to give attention to colleagues and customers; but no one pays us to give attention to our VIPs. In our work environment, we extend professionalism, business courtesy, honor hierarchy and protocols. And yet, when we enter our homes with our most intimate and immediate relationships, we sometimes forget they deserve that same level of treatment, and more.

It is common for my clients to admit they take their family and close relationships for granted. Many leaders work hard to create a lifestyle for the people they love. Yet, given time at night or on the weekend or vacation, they are still making work more important than the people with whom they share their lives. Too many people assume those closest to them will always be around and that they will always be forgiving. Sadly, that's often not the case. When the people we care about at home don't feel seen and heard, they often seek attention somewhere else, in online conversations or even other relationships.

I don't want you sitting at the hospital bedside, across the table from your former partner with your lawyer at your side, or at the funeral of a friend wishing you'd spent more time with people you love or created more memories or had deeper conversations. I don't want you to live in regret of what you could, should, or would have done. I want you to make a choice today to give intentional attention to the people you care about.

Who Are Your Personal VIPs?

There are three categories of people in your personal life who require your attention:

1. *Intimate*—the people closest to you
2. *Immediate*—your friends and family
3. *Community*—online and offline groups, including spiritual, physical, and educational groups

Each of these categories requires a different investment of energy and time. When time is scarce, those in your intimate and immediate category become your priority. When time is abundant, you can expand to those in your community.

Exercise:

List three people in your intimate circle who need your attention this week:

_____

_____

_____

List three people in your immediate circle that need your attention this month:

_____

_____

_____

List three people in your community that need your attention this year:

_____

_____

_____

You know who matters to you, but do they know they matter to you?

When is the last time you:

- Told your partner how much you appreciate them?
- Stopped to play a game or read a book with your child?
- Surprised someone close to you with their favorite treat—flowers, chocolates, ice cream, or a book by their favorite author?

- Called your mum or your dad or your godparent, just to say *hello*?

Showing people they are important is a series of little actions with big impact. Throughout this chapter, I'll give you tips and strategies to demonstrate to people that they matter to you.

Who Needs Your Attention at Work?

Human beings want to be seen and heard. My friend Donovan reminded me of this when he grabbed my cheeks in his little hands and demanded, "Neen, listen with your eyes!" The people we work with are no exception. And just like the people in our personal lives, when those we work with don't feel seen and heard, they seek attention somewhere else—usually with other companies!

Imagine what it would be like if you entered your boss's office and they stepped away from their computer, put their phone on silent, and put it away. As you spoke, they looked at you, giving you their undivided attention. They waited until you finished speaking, then asked a question or two, showing they had listened with their ears, their eyes, and their mind. Imagine how that would feel. Would you feel that your boss was investing in you? Taking time to really hear and address your concerns?

Does your team get your attention when they enter your office?

If not, I hope you know what your first strategy is! Here's a challenge to you: When your team members, boss, colleagues, and customers come to you, can you give them your undivided, intentional attention? Can you stop what you're doing and look them in the eye? Can you be more deliberate about who you want and need to pay attention to?

When is the last time you:

- Told a client or customer how much you appreciate them?
- Surprised your team with donuts or cookies?
- Emailed a team member a message of congratulations on a project they completed?
- Acknowledged a coworker's important holiday, such as Greek Independence Day, Chinese New Year, or Rosh Hashanah?

Organizations spend untold amounts of time, energy, and money on programs and initiatives to retain their talent. A Global Workforce Study by Towers Watson found that retaining employees has more to do with the quality of the work experience than compensation: "While some elements—like pay—affect both attraction and retention, the latter depends far more on the *quality of employees' relationship with their managers*, their trust in senior leadership and their ability to manage stress on the job." The study also found that employees who feel appreciated tend to be less stressed, have a better sense of belonging, and feel like they have better control over their lives.

In a fascinating article for *Forbes*, author and leadership advisor Mike Myatt lists 10 reasons top talent leaves. It's no surprise that 8 of the 10 reasons are directly tied to a leader's commitment to give team members intentional attention. Intentional attention is not only free but it is also one of the most powerful ways to keep your team members happy, engaged, and productive.

Who Are Your Professional VIPs?

There are four groups of people you work with who require your attention:

1. *Your team*—direct and virtual reports, people you are responsible for developing.

2. *Your boss*—person/or group to whom you are accountable for delivering results.

3. *Your colleagues*—people you collaborate with throughout the organization.

4. *Your clients*—these include internal client groups and external customers.

Each of these groups requires a variety of attention, brainpower, and time investment. Consider similar guidelines to our recommendations for your personal attention. When time is scarce, your team and boss become your priority. When time is abundant, you can expand to colleagues and clients.

The Other Kind of VIPs

Early in my career, I determined there are two types of people: VIPs and VDPs. VIPs are *very inspiring people*. When you are with them, you enjoy life. You're inspired to do better and to be a better person. VDPs are *very draining people*. VDPs suck your time and energy. You don't enjoy their company and dread seeing them.

In both your personal and professional life, whenever possible, choose to be surrounded with VIPs and eliminate VDPs. If eliminating your VDPs is not an option, minimize time with them. Spending time with VIPs motivates and invigorates you and accelerates your productivity. The opposite happens when you spend time with VDPs. Be deliberate in seeking out VIPs for your personal and professional life.

Do you have more VIPs or VDPs in your life? What can you do to spend more time with the VIPs and less time with the VDPs?

MANAGE YOUR COMMUNICATIONS WITH OTHERS
Use People's Names

Have you ever used your server's name at a restaurant and watched their eyes light up? Notice how they are more attentive to you? They check on you more frequently, make additional suggestions, and constantly refill your drink. You often want to leave them a bigger tip because you can tell they enjoyed waiting on you.

Using someone's name is a simple, no-cost, attention-giving strategy that makes people feel special. Dale Carnegie once wrote, "A person's name is the sweetest sound."

Watch people as their faces light up, they stand a little taller, and they smile more often when you use their name. When you notice someone by using their name, the situation shifts from a mere transaction to a transformational interaction. The other person feels seen and heard and responds positively.

Be a Fascinated Listener

So often in our attention-deficit society, we are chaotic listeners, listening to multiple things at once, but remembering little. Or we listen to respond, instead of listening to listen. In both cases, it's a waste of time and damages our relationships as well as others' perceptions of us. When we don't give intentional attention, it's also all too easy to misread someone's intentions. The results can be hurt feelings, disappointment, frustration, misunderstandings, misinterpreted requests, and mistakes.

Did you know the Hawaiian word for *listen* is *ho'olohe*? *Lohe* means "to listen, be attentive, obey, and listen intently." When *ho'o* is put in front of this word it turns it into an action word. We can learn from the beautiful language of the Hawaiian culture. Listening requires action.

Giving intentional attention means you aren't listening to other things, answering your email, or distracted by devices. It means you are looking intently at the person in front of you, maintaining eye contact, nodding, and showing them you are engaged in the conversation, even on teleconferences and video conferences. It's listening and looking for the real intention behind people's words and reading between the lines of what they are actually saying. When we actively listen, we get a more in-depth perception of what others are really trying to communicate.

In her book *Tell Me More on the Fine Art of Listening*, Brenda Ueland writes, "Listening is a magnetic and strange thing, a creative force. When people really listen to each other in a quiet, fascinated attention, the creative fountain inside each of us begins to spring and cast up new thoughts and unexpected wisdom." That quote reminds me of Tifphanie, a stylist at the Nordstrom store in King of Prussia, Pennsylvania. Tifphanie is one of our favorite people to work with, and she's an important part of our team. Executives love working with her. Her entire book of business is based on referrals. Every client will tell you she is one of the best listeners they have ever experienced.

When I asked Tifphanie about her listening skills, she shared, "When I listen to a client in a consultation for a stylist appointment, I'm not just listening to the details of their size and their height, I'm imagining who they are and it gives me an idea of their presence. I'm not just listening to what they say, but paying attention to how they say it, how they describe it, their body language. I zoom in on everything from words to emotions. I'm reading between the lines." This is why she is one of the most sought after stylists in Nordstrom.

How can you listen to others like Tifphanie?

Know Their Preferred Communication Style and Mode

Your family members, friends, coworkers, boss, and clients all have a preferred communication style and mode. You get to play detective and discover their style. Once you know their style (keep good notes), you can tailor how you communicate with them. Do they prefer you to get straight to the point or do they prefer small talk before getting down to business conversations? Do they need to understand why something needs to be done before they take action? Knowing preferences improve your relationships and allows you to be more efficient, and effective, when you communicate with them.

While managing large corporate teams in Australia, I kept detailed notes on every team member's and colleague's preferred style and mode of communication. We do the same thing today with every client. It sounds voluminous but it's really quite simple. Just make a note in each person's contact file in your digital address book. The information is always there when you need to contact that person.

One of my friends likes to use video calling apps, so we always see each other regardless of where we are in the world (and how unglamorous we look). This is an extra level of connection.

A client who is a human resources director prefers phone calls over email. Another client, a research executive in advertising, shares everything by text message. A managing partner in a law firm loves to meet face to face. Since this isn't always possible, we convinced him to try video technology so he still feels connected.

MANAGE YOUR RELATIONSHIPS WITH OTHERS

Step Away from the Device!

I'm always intrigued that so many people say their family is the most important thing to them, and yet they are constantly connected to their devices and engrossed in social media when they are with their family. Our attention is hyper-focused on our smartphones, smart devices, social media, and text messaging and not necessarily on what's important in the moment.

I leverage my electronic devices to the max as you'll see later in this chapter. And I love social media for staying in contact with friends and family around the globe, sharing fun client opportunities and participating in conversations with audience members from my speeches. We just need to make sure we are using these tools to enhance rather than damage our relationships with others. We can do that by being diligent in silencing our devices or turning them off to focus on the person we are with and by always using social media platforms to promote positive rather than negative messages.

Here are a few more tips to keep your device and social media usage in check:

- Play the game of *cell phone stack*—when eating a meal with friends, all cell phones go in a stack in the center of the table. The first person to reach for their cell picks up the check (that's a good incentive not to touch your devices).

- Before every meal, put your phone on silent so you can enjoy the company of others.

- Don't enter a room with your face in your device. Put away your phone beforehand to encourage connections with others.

- Use the elevator as a trigger: when you step in an elevator on your way to a meeting, silence your phone. When you leave the meeting and enter the elevator, change it back to normal mode.

- It should go without saying, but I'll say it again. Always put your device on silent and move it out of sight when having a conversation with someone. That includes phone calls and video conferences.

- If you don't want to unfriend someone on Facebook, and yet don't want to see their comments or feed, simply unfollow them.

- Unfriend people when you must. Yes, I do this. If you don't want to be associated with someone the easiest way to change the social media relationship is to unfriend them.

Create Significant Moments

Every day, explore ways to let people know that they matter to you. Remember, it is intention that makes attention valuable. Look for ways to create significant moments together. Who needs some intentional attention from you today? Try some of these ideas:

Intimate—the people closest to you

- Schedule a date night monthly with your partner; weekly is a bonus!

- Send balloons or a cookie or fruit bouquet, maybe even to their office.

- Know their favorite brand of ice cream, clothing, or fragrance and surprise them with a gift for no reason.

- Send a photo of an experience you have shared in a text message.

- Create a short video and text it to them.

- Conduct a family meeting to understand everyone's movements for the week ahead.

Immediate—your friends and family

- Create a slide show of photographs and share it. Huge bonus points if you turn it into a keepsake photo book.

- Plan a monthly get together to celebrate each month's birthdays (for example, get together in May to celebrate all those in the group with May birthdays).

- Buy tickets to an event and surprise them.

- Schedule a vacation and involve everyone with the planning.

- Organize and put on a family reunion.

- Schedule regular *guys' night out* or *girls' trips*.

- Send a handwritten birthday card or note of encouragement.

- Know the causes that are important to them and donate to those causes in their honor for their birthday

Community—online and offline groups, acquaintances, even strangers!

- Post a note on a social media platform to congratulate others on an achievement.

- Write a note thanking someone else for volunteering to take on a leadership role with a committee, team, or organization.

- Send an update of a project success by email and copy all relevant parties.

- Use a fundraiser to gather people for a cause.

- Volunteer for a cause you believe in, and serve on a committee or their board.

- Offer to speak at an event and highlight a project you are working on with others.

- Compliment your barista.

Coworkers—team members, boss, colleagues, clients

- Share with your boss something a colleague did to help you achieve an objective.

- Share a book you read and enjoyed, or buy a copy for the whole team, or give your copy to someone.

- Share a podcast on an area of their interest.

- Pick up your team's favorite coffee order.

- Thank your security guard and janitorial staff.

- Serve on a board for an industry association or organization.

Video is a clever way to give personalized attention in a cluttered texting world. Videos allow others to hear your voice, see your face, and know you gave a little extra effort just for them.

For friends and special clients, I create a short video singing Happy Birthday and text it to them or very occasionally post online. (I don't have a great singing voice. It's high-pitched and I sound like I am five years old, but it's a fun way to let someone know I am thinking of them.) I've even been known to create a short video and text it as a response to a client inquiry!

Rev Your RAZ for Recognition

When we're overwhelmed, overstressed, and overtired, it's easy to look for and find the negatives around us. What if instead, we revved our RAZ (remember the *reticular activating system*?) to seek the positive? What if we focused on the great things happening around us and made a point of recognizing and sharing them with others?

Would you notice when your significant other brings you a cup of coffee or tea in the morning? Would you take the time to acknowledge the above-and-beyond effort a team member gave on a project?

Just as it's meaningful to understand and use others' communication modes, it's thoughtful to know how they like to receive recognition and then acknowledge them in their preferred method.

My job as a speaker demonstrates how much I enjoy public recognition, and obviously, not everyone is like me. My honey could think of nothing worse; he'd prefer private recognition for the accuracy of his work. A trip to the ice cream shop might work for one of your children, whereas a special book is a great reward for another. Some team members might like an in-person, verbal thank-you, while others value an email message to appreciate their good work. Some enjoy the satisfaction of being chosen to be involved in a special project or initiative, while others want to be recognized as the leader of that project or initiative.

IMPLEMENT SYSTEMIZED THOUGHTFULNESS

I try to make every person I am with the center of my attention at that point in time, which is often easier said than done. That's why I'm such a huge fan of systemized thoughtfulness. I know that sounds crazy to create a system for being kind, but hear me out. If you can associate attention-giving activities with your regular routine, you will develop a reputation as an individual and leader who gives intentional attention to others.

The secret to systemizing thoughtfulness is to associate an activity to form a habit. Here are four ways I have systematized my attention:

1. *Use your cell.* The tiny super computer you carry with you *everywhere* is a brilliant tool. Sure, you already know that. But how thoughtfully do you use it? Do you use it to proactively send a text to let someone know you thought of them, to randomly leave an encouraging voicemail, or to send a fun picture to remind a client or a team member of an event or conference you attended together?

   As a frequent flyer, my system is once I am in my seat on the airplane, I text people I care about (friends, family, and clients) before the crew asks us to switch off our phones. It's a deliberate practice that fills the time while waiting for the plane to take off with meaningful connections.

   Could you create a routine or system to consciously and deliberately reach out to people as part of your weekly activities?

2. *Carry notecards or stationery.* Have you noticed people rarely write thank-you letters anymore? (Except maybe

Jimmy Fallon.) The power of a personal note stands out in the world of electronic communications, status updates, and likes. There are many opportunities to thank people. We just need to create a system to always carry stamped company stationery and immediately take two to three minutes right then and there to write a quick note of appreciation.

We recommend to all our executives that they have personalized notecards to enhance their personal brand. A handwritten note on your personalized notecard creates a special moment for the receiver, a moment that matters to them. You may be surprised to learn many of your team members hold on to these notes and treasure not only the note, but the fact you took time from your busy schedule to notice what they did. Never underestimate the power of recognition through a handwritten note.

In every hotel room I leave a note of appreciation for housekeeping with the tip. When we check into hotels I often request the name of the General Manager so I can write a note complimenting any staff members who made my stay more enjoyable. Could you write a note for an amazing crew member who attended to you on your flight? Could you leave a note for the security guard who assists you every day?

Can you encourage your team to carry stamped stationery to send a note of appreciation after meeting with a client, or attending an industry conference, or receiving a new order from a customer?

3. *Send love notes.* That's what I call them. A note to someone you care about, just because. Consider leaving post-it notes around the house when you

travel. These messages remind someone you miss them (I do this often, and leave them on the bathroom mirror, on a pillow, in the fridge, and on our coffee machine). My honey finds these notes when I travel and smiles.

Here are some more ideas for love notes:

- Write a note and put it in your child's lunchbox or backpack.

- Slip a note of appreciation into your partner's briefcase or purse.

- Leave a note out for someone you share your home with when you are out doing errands, just to remind them they are important to you.

- Write a note to your parents to thank them for all that they have done for you and sacrificed.

- Send a card to your best friend to remind them you think of them often, even if you don't speak frequently.

Love notes are important to me. I love sending them, creating them, and receiving them. A really simple hack is to stock up on funny cards or notes the next time you're at the store so that you always have a collection available to send. I call this *planned spontaneity*—it's a spontaneous love note, and having the notes available and ready to go is the system.

4. *Use social media.* I am all about face-to-face attention for people who are important to us and that's not always possible with friends, family, coworkers, and clients spread across the globe. A phone or video call is a great option, and when that's not possible social media is a great tool to give attention to people you care about.

My system when I travel is to tweet about my client and the great service I receive while I am on the road. So when I am sitting on the plane, it's a great time to grab my phone, give a shout out, and know I am making someone smile. Every time I fly, I routinely tweet out something about my client, the speech I'm giving, or the destination I am excited to see. I am always impressed with how quickly (and how funny) American Airlines is at responding to my tweets. They always use my name and funny hash tags in their Twitter responses. They have systemized responsiveness to track posts they are tagged in and cleverly differentiate themselves from other airlines.

Could you post on social media about clients you enjoy working with? Can you spend a moment writing a quick positive comment on a friend's business Facebook page?

To systemize thoughtfulness with social media, my system is to manage it while drinking. No, not champagne, although that might make for some interesting posts. (On second thought, *never* post while drinking alcohol!) I mean drinking liquids. When I take a break to make a coffee or while I have my juice in the morning, this is when I zoom across all the social media platforms to give shoutouts on Twitter, likes on Facebook, and comments on Instagram. Tying a task with a regular activity, like drinking coffee, helps me to manage these online relationships.

Intentional attention begins with you. To lead and inspire every day requires you to be thoughtful and kind with yourself and others. Now, let's discover how you can better focus on the tasks and achievement of goals at work and help your team do the same.

Make Your Attention Pay

1. Who needs your attention today?

2. Who deserves your attention tonight?

3. Who isn't a high priority and can wait?

4. What is one action you can take today to show someone they matter to you?

PART THREE

Professionally—Be Productive

CHAPTER 5

Prioritize Your Priorities: Create
Significant Moments

I have a confession to make.

I have been known, on occasion, to write things on a to-do list just so I can cross them off. I know. It's a scary public admission from someone who is supposed to know a thing or two about productivity.

Do you ever do that? It's okay. You can tell me. No one else has to know. *Mmm hmm.* That's what I thought.

Why do we do that?

Because we want to know that we accomplished something today! At least one thing, no matter how small.

A common complaint of the leaders I work with is that they feel they spend significant time putting out metaphoric fires at work. They are pulled in multiple directions every day, permanently attached to their devices, running from one meeting to the next without a break. Their days are stolen by busy work, the demands of others, and unnecessary (and often poorly run) meetings. They work full speed from 7 a.m. to 7 p.m. and when they get to the end of the day, they have to sit down to complete their *real work*. Time for strategic thinking and working on important projects? There is none of that.

Can you relate?

You are not alone, but I'm not sure that's company you want to keep.

It's time to stop the crazy train! We need to take back our time, our attention, and our productivity—not only for ourselves, but for our teams, too.

Wouldn't it feel *ah-mazing* (one of my favorite words) to stop at 5:30 or 6 p.m., look back at the day, and feel a sense of accomplishment and purpose? Wouldn't it be invigorating to know that things you did today mattered? And wouldn't it just make you smile a big silly grin to know that you were done with work for the day and that you were off to focus on the people and passions most important to you?

It's not a dream. It is possible.

We consistently help clients achieve these same results. In our work together, we help them identify priorities, improve delegation of tasks, eliminate inefficient meetings, surgically audit email, and implement new systems to apply attention management strategies. Clients share with us that they get their time back, invest in their health, feel less stressed, achieve greater success, and are able to spend quality time with those they care about.

Our goal by the time you finish the professional attention section of this book is that you will be inspired to apply the many strategies shared to help you systemize your calendar management, overcome distractions, and commit to a healthy work environment where your team, leaders, and clients feel seen and heard by you. Let's talk about how to accelerate your productivity at work.

PACK YOUR HIGHEST PRIORITIES

When was the last time you went on a road trip? Planning the trip probably included deciding where to go, what route to take, what to visit, what to pack, what to wear, and the most important question, what snacks to take!

Imagine you are standing at your car, bags waiting to be placed in the boot (that's what we Aussies call the trunk). You look around you: suitcases, coolers, golf clubs, snacks, fishing rods, beach chairs, floats. You look back at the boot.

Which luggage do you pack first?

Some people are doers. These are the busy people. They grab the pieces closest to them and just start filling the boot. Whatever is left over at the end just gets left behind. They might end up at the beach with golf clubs and no beach chair, but, hey, they made it to the beach, didn't they? The analyzers step back, assess the space, look at the pieces, assess the space, and then look at the pieces again. For them, it's like playing a game of *Tetris*. Can they make it all fit nicely and neatly? They will still be standing there analyzing while the rest of us are long gone.

Then there are those people who take the conscious and deliberate approach: "Which items are most important for where I'm going? Put those in first." They start with the suitcase (pretty important unless you're headed to a nudist colony), then add the snacks (like that's even a question). *Hmmm*—golf clubs, fishing rod, or beach chair? Now, we have to make some tough choices. What is most important? What activities are my highest priorities? These intentional souls usually get just about every piece in the car, and any that are left behind won't be missed because they took the time to consider their priorities and act accordingly.

Our day is like a road trip. The busy doers are just trying to get something, anything, done so they can cross it off a list.

However, this strategy is pointless. Even though it temporarily makes them feel good to get something completed, they will have a tough time achieving their goals. The analyzers suffer from analysis paralysis (no surprise there). The opposite of the doers, they get nothing done because they are so overwhelmed by the enormity of it all. There's so much to do on any given day, where do they start? How will they get it all done? So, they do nothing.

Those with intentional attention spend 15 minutes each morning deciding their top three priorities for the day. They know where they are going—their long-term goals—and they know how their daily goals will help them reach their ultimate destination. They accomplish their non-negotiable priorities first, and then fill in with lower-level priorities. They maximize their time and attention, and each day moves them closer to achieving their goals.

Which one are you? How do you prioritize your priorities?

When we operate in an attention-deficit mentality, combined with the Over Trilogy (overwhelmed, overstressed, and overtired), it's often easy to forget we need to focus on our priorities first. Our to-do lists keep growing and we accept every request, but that just makes us busy, not productive.

What are your highest priorities? Can you list your top five personal priorities for the next 30 days? What are your top 10 priorities for this year?

You have 1,440 minutes each day. Once your time is spent, you don't get it back. Are you investing them or are you wasting them? To make the most of every moment, you have to know who and what to focus on.

You don't have time to do everything; you only have time to do what matters.

Your Top 10

When I lived in Sydney, every January I booked an appointment with myself. I'd sit at the same table at Sheraton on the Park, enjoy the gorgeous view, order a glass of champagne, and sit with a notepad and a pen. I'd pull out last year's goals and do a gap analysis. Which ones did I achieve? What needed to be changed? Then I would set new priorities for the coming year. I did this every year for 10 years. I miss that table.

Could you create an appointment with yourself this year to start a new tradition? Set aside a time and place and create your top 10 priorities for your year. Then every year, revisit that list to measure your success.

PROTECT YOUR TIME

When it comes to improving productivity, many people believe the issue is time. I'll acknowledge, I used to think the same thing. Then I realized we are trying to fix something that is fixed, instead of managing something that is flexible.

Time is fixed; we can't change that. We all get the same number of minutes in a day. No one gets more. Yet, I bet you know certain people who seem to be getting it all done—and doing it fairly easily without a lot of drama and stress. These people have figured out it isn't about time.

Time is fixed, but attention is flexible. Which means it's not about time management; it's about attention management.

We don't have a time management crisis; we have an attention management crisis.

While we can't control time, we can protect what time we have. Our attention-deficit society constantly conspires to steal our time and attention. We have to shield and safeguard our time so that we can direct our intentional attention into more strategic activities, such as the priorities that matter most.

I love systems. Systems create freedom, and freedom is a good thing! In this section, we are going to look at defense systems to help you proactively guard your time and attention.

Systemize Your Calendar

One of the most powerful yet simple systems to protect your time is to systemize your calendar. Doing so will focus your attention to achieve your most strategic objectives.

Many leaders tell me that meetings are the biggest culprit in stealing their time, so let's address this head on. Did you know you can say *no* to a meeting? It's true. You can decline an invitation to a meeting. Of course, there are some meetings you will always have to attend, but those are far fewer than you might think. When invited to any meeting, determine if it's necessary for you to attend:

- Ask for the agenda in advance to understand your involvement. If no agenda is available (a sure sign the facilitator is not prepared), decline the meeting.
- Check the agenda to see if you need to attend the whole meeting or just your agenda items.
- Question the meeting purpose and how you will add value.

If you determine your attendance is not needed, be brave—decline the meeting!

Here are more strategies to systemize your calendar:

- *Create a personal daily strategic 15-minute appointment*—Take this time to determine your top three non-negotiable activities you must complete before you sleep tonight. Several years ago, I challenged an executive leadership team at Comcast to invest 15 minutes of their attention every day in a strategic appointment. They saw awesome results, becoming the highest performing team in their region. Their shared increased focus allowed them to prioritize completion of strategic objectives and invest in their people development instead of being distracted by everyday busyness.

- *Schedule your morning routine*—We outlined this routine in detail in Chapter 3. It's critical that you get this on your calendar so that phone calls or meetings don't encroach on this important time.

- *Assign certain activities to specific days of the week*—This system has you group regular activities together to maximize productivity and minimize distractions. Will it work seamlessly with every week in the same way? No, but with a system, your team or assistant can schedule meetings on designated days. We worked with a financial services executive to design her ideal week. Here is what hers looked like. Yours, of course, will be different:

    - *Monday*—meet with team members, senior leadership, and her boss in the office.

    - *Tuesday to Thursday*—industry and vendor networking events, client appointments, presentation preparation, and travel. These days were spent outside the office and included a work-from-home day.

- *Friday*—As she enjoyed being home for weekends, any meetings were local and never scheduled to finish later than 5 PM. If no meetings were scheduled, she focused on strategizing for the upcoming week and catching up on administrative work.

- *Schedule* no-talk *days*—My best friend Meg manages multiple companies, raises my two gorgeous god-daughters, volunteers in her community, and enjoys working with her clients. She discovered that on days she doesn't talk to anyone, she's massively productive. So, she started scheduling no-talk days—days with no appointments, which are dedicated to strategy and achieving goals. As an extrovert, I found this strategy especially helpful. Could you do this once a quarter to make more progress toward your bigger goals?

- *Schedule service days*—I allocate one day a month on my calendar for pro bono assistance to people in my industry who need help. Could you add a service day to your calendar?

- *Time block*—Schedule space in your calendar for strategy, email review, meetings, social media engagement, and personal time.

- *Create visual recognition systems*—Use color-coding to simplify your life. My calendar uses a variety of colors to show speaking, travel, consulting, personal appointments, and administration and business development.

- *Block out personal time* in advance and honor the appointment.

What Is Your Ideal Week?

How can you group regular activities to maximize productivity and minimize distractions?

Monday—

Tuesday—

Wednesday—

Thursday—

Friday—

What is the second biggest time thief behind meetings? You guessed it. *Email.*

Defend Against Your Biggest Distraction

According to McKinsey, 28% of a person's workday is spent checking email. That's over one-quarter of your entire business day! It's a wonder any of us get anything done.

Other studies show that 26% of employees admit email is their number one distraction. Implement these strategies to defend against email distractions:

- *Invest time in 15 minutes increments*—According to the University of British Columbia, limiting your reading of email to three times per day reduces stress and distractions by 47%, boosting productivity and focus. When you do check email, only spend 15 dedicated, focused minutes at a time. Set the timer on your phone to answer as many as you can in that concentrated period of time. Giving your email your full attention at specified points throughout the day will save you hours of scrolling and prevent distracted, half-answered emails.

- *Don't reinvent the wheel*—Create custom email templates to quickly and thoughtfully respond to regular or repeated requests.

- *Use the latest apps to do the work for you*—Go to neenjames .com/extras for my favorite Attention Resources to help you implement these email defense systems:

  - *Unplug from the unwanted*—There are apps available that will unsubscribe you from unwanted subscriptions filling up your inbox.

  - *Block it out*—Use a distraction management app to block social media sites and email. It's the Internet version of a *do not disturb* sign and ideal for creating uninterrupted time.

  - *Create shortcuts*—Smart apps create shortcuts for regularly used responses, words, and templates.

  - *Bounce back*—A nifty app allows you to bounce emails back to yourself when you want to answer them and schedule delivery for another time.

- *Leverage your out of office message*—If you have an assistant (physical or virtual), leverage your out of office message to divert email requests to your assistant to handle. Be sure to let people know that they can contact your assistant in your absence and provide contact information. Imagine what you could do with your attention if your assistant were able to handle even 25% of your emails. You can also leverage your out of office message to generate attention and show you are being thoughtful with your response. See the examples shared in the call-out box for more.

Remember, most emails you receive are requests from people who want your time and attention to accomplish their objectives. Email is an important tool. When used well it assists communications, but if not managed it kills productivity. Don't be the leader who gives half-responses and sends emails full of spelling errors or emoticons. Be an influential communicator. For the next 24 hours, decide you will be more intentional with every email response.

Leverage Your Out of Office Message

Use this communication touch point to grab your readers' attention quickly with a fun, even quirky, response. Every time we are out of the office, away from our email (which is several times each week), we change the message to something fun. Some clients even know I am out of the office and still send me messages, just to see what they will get in response. Here are a few client favorites. What could you do with your out of office message?

SUBJECT: I'm watching Ferraris race around the track today—in Austin, such a cool city.

G'Day,

You may not know this about me, but I love Formula One events (go Ferrari) and try to attend a different event each year. Today I am in Austin so Maria is monitoring our email and can help you with anything you might need (she really is the Queen of Neen).

Looking forward to connecting with you when I get back,

SUBJECT: So excited to be speaking for a client—in Hawaii!

G'Day, Hello, Aloha,

This week I am speaking for a phenomenal client in Hawaii and taking a few days off to enjoy a little break. My little sister from Australia is even flying in to meet me! Maria is monitoring our email and can help you with anything you might need (she really is the Queen of Neen).

SUBJECT: I am hiding—locked away to finish my manuscript!

G'Day,

Today I am in the final stages of finishing my manuscript for my new book with Wiley and I am beyond excited (I have a great team)! Maria is monitoring our email and can help you with anything you might need (she really is the Queen of Neen). I will be offline this week but she's ready to respond!

Looking forward to connecting with you really soon,

Outsource Your Life

To increase productivity professionally, outsource personal activities that don't require your intentional attention. What is the biggest time and attention drain in your personal life? Could one of these be the solution?

- Hire virtual assistants who will perform tasks for both your work and personal life.
- Use a driver service for airport travel to participate in conference calls or catch up on email and personal calls.

- Hire cleaning services to give you more time with people you care about.
- Find a dry cleaner that drops off and delivers laundry.
- Try one of the many meal and grocery delivery services that offer easily assembled ingredients or premade meals to share with your loved ones.
- Use a personal shopper or stylist who can create wardrobes for you and send them to your home or office.

Are you sitting there reading this thinking, *I can't hire a personal shopper* or *I can't afford a cleaning service*? You might be right—or you might be wrong. Did you know retail personal shoppers work on commission? They are paid by the store, not by you. Do stylists and meal delivery services cost more money? Yes. And they are worth it.

You are worth investing in. Your personal brand will be stronger when you invest in clothes that make you look and feel confident. You will get more time back with people you care about if you consider outsourcing activities that take you away from them like cleaning, shopping, and errands. This is a situation where you actually can buy time and give yourself more hours in the day.

GUARD YOUR FOCUS

Entrepreneur, entertainer, and philanthropist Oprah Winfrey is worth about $3 billion as of this writing. She must know a thing or two about success. "Energy is the essence of life," she says. "Every day you decide how you are going to use it by knowing what you want and what it takes to reach that goal, and by maintaining focus."

Just as we must proactively protect our time, we must also protect our focus if we want to have the mental and physical energy available to accelerate our productivity.

"No" Is a Complete Sentence

Top producers and exceptional earners are strategic thinkers. They know their bandwidth at any given time. In order to be on top of their game, they keep their sights on the high-priority activities that will take them closer to their goals. How can you do that more often?

Say *no*—often!

Warren Buffett said, "The difference between successful people and *very* successful people is that very successful people say no to almost everything."

Figure out what to say *no* to, so you can say *yes* to what really matters. That's when you know you're investing intentional attention. In his book *Anything You Want*, Derek Sivers points out, "When you say no to most things you leave room in your life to throw yourself completely into that rare thing that makes you say, 'hell yeah!'"

I love that! Your life deserves a whole lot more *hell yeah* moments.

When we say yes to everything, we don't leave room for opportunities that might be more productive, fun, or rewarding. Saying no can lead to a bigger yes:

- Eliminate distractions to stay focused on goals.
- Use resources more effectively (time and talent).
- Travel a path to be a more focused leader.
- Narrow choices, thus keeping focus crystal clear.
- Preserve energy (physical and mental).

- Fail faster (yes, that's a good thing).
- Fail smarter (love a great learning curve).
- Be more honest (how many times did you really want to say no before?)

Why are we so uncomfortable saying no, even when we know saying yes is not a good investment of our attention? The reasons might include: you want to be helpful or a team player; you want the accolades of being a *yes* person; or you like staying crazy busy. Saying no when people ask you to help them with projects or attend an event you don't want to doesn't make you rude, or a bad friend, or a bad team member. It makes you focused and keeps you on track.

"But Neen, how do I say *no*?" Let me help you.

"Thank you for thinking of me for that important project. I'd love to be part of the team. Which of these priorities do you want me to stop working on so I can join you?"

"Thank you for your kind invitation. I am unable to join you." Or *"Thank you for your kind invitation, I have another commitment."*

"Thank you for thinking of me for that committee. I'd love to be involved. I will be finished this current project in two weeks. May I reconnect with you to discuss this further?"

That's it. Don't overcomplicate it. Don't throw excuses or fibs at it. Just say, kindly and politely, "No, thank you."

Once you determine the priorities to which you want to say yes, you can say no to others and focus on what's most important. When in doubt, ask yourself, "What most needs my attention?"

Say no to the things that don't take you closer to your goals, get you excited, make you want to jump out of bed, or move you forward. That way there is room to say yes to all the things that do.

Bring Back the Gatekeeper

A gatekeeper is a team member who works closely with a leader and who is renowned for asking questions, making it difficult to get an appointment, managing the leader's business objectives, and keeping the boss focused to achieve those objectives. This role keeps you focused on your priorities and helps manage distractions. Gatekeepers represent a formidable defense system.

In my corporate career, direct reports knew my gatekeeper could speak on my behalf and regularly start meetings. She was known for protecting my time and project focus. When I started my entrepreneurial adventure, my first hire was a gatekeeper. When I relocated from Sydney to the United States, with no clients, no income (no money to buy shoes), and no speaking engagements, I hired a gatekeeper. It's that vital to your productivity and success.

You can hire virtual assistants to be your gatekeeper. In our office, Maria started as a virtual assistant, only working a few hours a month. Now, 10-plus years later, she is the most vital member of our team and has been affectionately named *Queen of Neen* by clients and colleagues who adore her. We could never do what we do without her.

If you want to accelerate your productivity, get a gatekeeper. Perhaps you could *share* a gatekeeper with another leader within your organization. Or, hire a virtual assistant. If all else fails, be your own gatekeeper:

- Systemize your calendar and stick to it. Calendar management is one of the most effective tools of a gatekeeper. Go back and reread the section on calendar management and then do it!
- Schedule teleconferences or videoconferences instead of face-to-face meetings to avoid wasted travel time.
- Scan emails and limit answers to quick responses.

- Coordinate travel at convenient times with the most direct flights staying at the most convenient hotel.

- Unsubscribe from any and all magazines, blogs, and newsletters you don't read

- Color-code files for easy reference and quick access to important materials.

- Create a catalog system for your important files online and offline.

Great outsourcing services are also available for everything from research to graphic design.

> Go to neenjames.com/extras for my favorite Attention Resources.

Fight Decision Fatigue

According to research, every day we make somewhere between 23,000 and 35,000 decisions that allow us to function. The majority of these decisions are made subconsciously. A Columbia University study, led by decision researcher Sheena Iyengar, shared that the average American makes approximately 70 conscious decisions every day.

When we make decisions or choices, we are flexing the executive function portion of our brain. The brain works like a muscle. It can become stronger. But when our brain has to make many decisions (big and small), it becomes less effective.

With the number of decisions we have to make every day and the volume of information we have to process, our brains tend to get overworked. The result is that it's harder for our brains to focus and pay attention. When we are tired and under stress we might also be more challenged to invest our attention wisely. This is why we tend to tune out (maybe watch TV) and avoid meaningful conversations with people at the end of a long, hectic, decision-filled workday.

One way to protect our focus and improve our attention is to reduce the amount of information we have to process and the number of decisions we have to make each day. There are well-documented examples of world and business leaders (Steve Jobs, Mark Zuckerberg) who created routines and daily disciplines to minimize their decision making, thus allowing their attention to be focused on the most impactful decisions each day.

Former President Barack Obama believes the simple act of making decisions degrades one's ability to focus on what matters. "You'll see I wear only gray or blue suits.... I'm trying to pare down decisions. I don't want to make decisions about what I'm eating or wearing because I have too many other decisions to make."

You can use the same strategy. I call it "Sort on Sundays." Each Sunday, invest about 15 minutes to plan your wardrobe for the week. Determine what activities you have on your calendar and set aside the outfits you need for each. I learned this technique from Megan Kristel, founder of Kristel Closets. Consider allocating a section of your closet in which to place these items. Invest your attention on Sunday so you can give it more intentionally throughout the week.

Henry David Thoreau once said, "Our life is frittered away by detail. Simplify. Simplify."

Where can you simplify to free up brainpower and pay more attention to the people, priorities, and passions that matter?

Discipline Your Use of Devices and Social Media

Sound familiar? Do you see a common thread here? Our obsession with our devices and social media bleed into almost every aspect of our lives. They affect how we give intentional attention to ourselves and to others and how productive we and our teams are at work.

When I interviewed Fred Stutzman, the creator and founder of the Freedom app, I asked why he designed a site-blocking app. "Being productive in our age of distraction is one of the most difficult challenges we face," he said. "There are so many forces competing for our attention, and few easy solutions to this problem. We created Freedom to enable people to fight back by easily blocking distractions on their devices so they can get work done. We're proud to have helped hundreds of thousands of people achieve their goals—and work on what truly matters."

I truly would never have written this book if it wasn't for his app. It's ironic that it was difficult for the attention expert to focus on writing a book on attention! But it speaks to how difficult it is for all of us to fight these distractions.

Protect your focus and your attention with these device management strategies:

- As we discussed in Chapter 3 regarding your nighttime routine, keep your devices out of your bedroom. Period.

- Forward your cell phone to your office phone so only one phone rings during the day.

- Install an app that tracks how much time you spend on your cell phone and be prepared to be shocked!

- Turn off every notification and reminder to avoid distractions and interruptions.

- Use the do-not-disturb function or switch your device to airplane mode to allow you to focus on completing work.

- Place your cell phone in your office drawer when working on a project to accelerate dedicated focus.

- Remove unnecessary apps from your cell phone so you don't waste time (and space) checking and updating them.

- Use site-blocking software or apps to stay focused.

To break the cycle of our unhealthy attention habits, try these social media strategies:

- Do a daily social media "drive-by." Discipline yourself by setting time limits for your social media usage. I invest 15 minutes in the morning quickly reviewing all social media platforms while drinking my morning coffee. I like, retweet, comment, share memories, add to discussion groups, and repost across platforms including Facebook, Instagram, Twitter, and LinkedIn.

- Use only one device to check social media sites when you are working on a big project. This allows you to keep your computer for work-related functions and your cell phone or tablet for social media checking. While writing this book, I tried to limit social media to only my cell phone (instead of my computer) to stay focused on writing.

- Install the time-savers from your browser. I use the Facebook News Feed Eradicator application on my Chrome browser (at the time of printing it was revolutionary and time-saving for me). It does exactly what the name suggests. You won't see any of the Facebook feed and you can manually enter people's names or groups to get an update.

- If you are brave, delete social media apps from your cell phone and notice how much more productive you are.

Let's use technology for good to create new systems to change our habits.

Check out all of my favorite Attention Resources at neenjames.com/extras.

Do a Digital Detox

I thought it would be easy: Spend a holiday weekend offline. I switched off my iPhone, iPad, and computer (no email or social media). I also told my honey I was doing a digital detox so I could be held accountable and not tempted to cheat.

Embarking on a self-imposed digital detox for three days was enlightening. I felt so productive. I caught up on professional reading and organized office files. A five-mile walk without music and distraction allowed me to notice the sounds of the wildlife and feel the sun on my skin. And guess what? My world was still there when I returned. No relationships were ruined; my emails were still there; and my notifications on social media had increased but were still manageable. I felt light and calm, connected, and present.

Are you brave enough to try a digital detox? Maybe you can't do three days. Could you try three hours?

Choose a timeframe that works for you. Notify friends and family you will be offline, especially if they are used to connecting with you in this way. Turn off notifications and any sounds that will distract you, and put away devices. Then, go experience freedom!

Jim Rohn said, "Success is nothing more than a few simple disciplines practiced every day." He's right, especially in how, and when, we are deliberate and disciplined with our attention.

Most of you reading this don't have someone standing over your shoulder, watching your every move, to see if you are answering emails, checking your Facebook status, or creating a client proposal. As a leader, you are 100% accountable for the choices you make and the actions you take. Today, decide that you will be more focused and committed with how you give your attention, so you can be a person of integrity who does what they say they will do.

Now that we've discussed how we can be personally responsible for investing our attention and accelerating our productivity, let's find out how you can help your team do the same. In Chapter 6, we will show you how attention pays for you, your team, and the organization when everyone is focused on their most important work.

Make Your Attention Pay

1. What systems do you need to implement in your calendar this week?
2. Where do you need to say no this week?
3. Can you be your own gatekeeper this month?

CHAPTER 6

Create a Culture of Attention: Stop the Madness

Consider this compelling statistic from a recent Cornerstone survey:

68% of U.S. full-time employees are suffering from work overload.

The Cornerstone survey also found that 6 in 10 (61%) employees believe that work overload is most harmful to their productivity. "This amplifies the frustrating paradox of today's hyper-connected workforce: the more overworked people are, the more they have to work longer hours; the longer they work, the less productive they become; and the less productive they become, the longer they must work."

Does all of this sound familiar? Remember the Over Trilogy? Turns out you aren't the only one who might be overwhelmed, overstressed, and overtired. More than likely, your team members are, too!

No matter whether you lead a team at work, serve as a board member, or volunteer for a cause you believe in, a key aspect of your role is to help others be more productive so they can give intentional attention to their customers. When team members are productive and focused to achieve results at work, your company will be more profitable, with higher customer satisfaction scores and increased sales.

Our goal for you when you finish this chapter is to be inspired to apply these strategies to create a productive and healthy work environment and a culture that inspires teams to collaborate on projects, complete deadlines, and practice kindness. And, you will see how well attention pays in terms of increased accountability and ultimately, accelerated profitability for your organization.

SHOW THEM THE PATH AND THEN EMPOWER THEM TO TAKE IT

Your team doesn't have time to do everything, only time to do what matters. (Sound familiar? It's as true for them as it is for you.)

What matters most to you and your team?

Do *you* know?

Do *they* know?

A critical skill for every leader is helping team members set and manage priorities. Having clearly defined priorities and expectations are the foundation of productivity. If your team is not on track, that's your responsibility, not theirs. You are often privy to conversations with senior leaders outlining what's most important for the year as well as the quarterly focus. To accelerate productivity with your team, translate your understanding of these priorities into tangible strategies they can apply in their everyday activities.

Here are some strategies to help you give intentional attention to your team's priorities:

- *Monitor your team's individual objectives*—It's your role as a leader to help the team pay attention to the measurements of your business. Many organizations establish *Key Performance Indicators* (KPIs). These are measurable values that demonstrate how effectively you or your company is achieving key business objectives. If you want to help your team focus monthly, weekly, and even daily, monitoring KPIs is a great strategy for continual accountability. Organizations set the big picture goals and objectives, but leaders must monitor how their team is working toward them. You could meet with your team to create *Critical Success Factors* (CSF) together. Think of these as elements that will help the team strategy be successful. Once you are clear on the success factors, you can define personalized KPIs with metrics.

- *Break it down*—Annual goals can be overwhelming. Work with your team to break them down into smaller, achievable priorities, tasks, and actions to be completed monthly or even weekly. This will help them know where to focus their talents and energy. Print them out so each team member can see them daily to direct their attention (especially on the days you find yourself distracted and wasting time).

- *Review progress*—Make one-on-one appointments with every team member to meet regularly to review progress against KPIs. Discuss their project load and assess how they are prioritizing their workload. Create an environment where they feel comfortable seeking your advice to help them re-sort, reorganize, or release projects to ensure they are focused on achieving the most important deadlines and deliverables.

- *Stay connected*—As a leader, it is your responsibility to know the status of your team's projects, goals, and objectives. Work together to implement systems for them to keep you updated on their progress in between your one-on-ones. You will always be ready to provide updates to your boss and be able to promote them and their work to others in your organization.

- *Empower them*—It's easy to fall into micromanaging or looking over your team's shoulders. These are fast tracks, however, to mediocrity. Encourage your team members to take ownership of their projects, their processes, their time, their decisions, their careers, and their choices. And then let them! When they take ownership, they sharpen their focus on the things that are most important, and when that happens in an organization, everyone gets better.

- *Leverage and develop team member strengths*—Invest in training and development for your team to ensure they have all the skills and motivation required to do their jobs. Invest time with each team member to establish annual training goals and build a plan together to support them. This plan might include online training, attendance at conferences, subscriptions to industry journals, listening to recommended podcasts, or obtaining continuing education credits.

- *Set it free*—We have all been guilty of investing our time and attention in a project or activity secretly knowing it may not work or desperately hoping somehow it will all be okay. Be prepared to stop projects and make tough decisions when necessary. Be willing to acknowledge that some client requests are unreasonable, some deadlines not achievable, and some requests are just ridiculous. As a leader, you may need to help others *set it free*.

I have encouraged many clients to get comfortable with setting projects (and people) free.

- *Fail fast and move on*—If you want to be more productive, learn how to fail fast and move on. Celebrate any projects that fail and encourage team members to focus on what works, what gives them the highest ROA (return on attention), and keep moving. Don't dwell on failures. Debrief them, and then move on.

As a leader, you help your team set priorities. You also set the tone for success in the workplace. If your team members aren't at the top of their game in terms of health and wellness, it affects productivity, profitability, and your ability to compete at a high level. Let's see how you can help create the ideal environment for success.

CULTIVATE AN ENVIRONMENT WHERE PRODUCTIVITY THRIVES

You and your team invest a significant amount of time working each day. You spend 50 percent of your total waking hours each day at work. That is 23 percent of your total time during a 50-year working life. That's huge!

Wouldn't it make sense to create environments where people can be productive and give intentional attention to what matters most in your organization? Where people know they are valued and because of that, they are inspired to contribute more? While we're at it, why not also create environments where people enjoy coming to work and collaborating as a team? Productivity is the prize.

Create an Agile Work Culture

Meeting the challenges of today's workforce and competitive markets means strong leaders have to pay attention to detail and lead with a new kind of flexibility. I'm often called by clients to help them determine what a shift in flexibility would mean to their work environment and team members and create a process to make it happen. Here are some strategies I use with my clients to create an agile work culture:

- *Tip your hat to technology.* As I've said, I don't think technology is evil. It is an amazing tool (that we need to be able to manage) that allows people to work from home, email from airplanes, telecommute, and patch into meetings on the other side of the world with ease. Leverage that ability.

- *Establish work–life boundaries.* As a leader, you are a role model for technology use. You set the tone and informally demonstrate how you want team members to respond. Don't email team members late at night unnecessarily; you are stealing minutes from their families. Don't expect the team to *just dial in* to a conference call if they are on vacation; you are stealing memories from their loved ones. Stop it. Today, make a decision to create guidelines with your team of how you will respect work–life boundaries.

- *Remove the burden of guilt.* Do you have a team member who would be best served working from home or someone who needs to shift hours to make childcare work? The goal is to get the work done. Often, you have flexibility regarding where that work takes place and at what time of day. Remove the guilt, increase the flexibility, and watch the workflow accelerate.

- *Reevaluate and customize the work environment.* To increase flexibility and productivity, try to match team members' needs with their workspace. Who needs a quiet space to work? Can you do away with cubicles for those team members? Who works better with collaboration? Do they have an area to brainstorm? Can you consider a more open workspace for them? When you reconsider all the components of your work environment and directly match them up to what your team needs to be at their best, you'll create a space for people to work at their highest and best capacity.

- *Create a distraction-free zone.* Dedicate an area of workspace or a time period each day that is declared *distraction-free.* That means no meetings and no interruptions from peers or management within that space or during that time. Everyone (you, too!) has the freedom to complete work, create, and stay on task. For some organizations, implementing just this one idea changes the whole dynamic of their workdays by decreasing stress and increasing productivity. Try it.

- *Design over process.* Start today to question the design of how things have always been done. Look for opportunities to rethink old processes, improve skills, fuel innovation, and encourage positive change. The best place to start? Your team. Listen to them, learn from them, and then use that insight to challenge processes and improve systems.

Creating a Culture of Intentional Attention

Johnson & Johnson (J & J) is a client I deeply admire, and a great example of intentional attention personally, professionally, and globally. Their credo focuses on the impact their products and services make on individuals, the company, and the wider community.

As one of the largest healthcare companies in the world with over a billion patients using their products every day, Alex Gorsky, chairman of the board and chief executive officer, believes in ensuring his team members are healthy, too.

In an interview with Arianna Huffington, founder of the *Huffington Post* and author of *Thrive*, Gorsky shares his belief that healthier employees do better, do more, and help more people in their community. He pointed out that as they do more work in the area of wellness at J & J, employee engagement scores go up.

He also challenges his leadership team to be healthier, sharing that leaders too often put their own health in the back seat. His philosophy: *Who you are as a person says who you are as a leader. If you are a tired person, you are going to be a tired and boring leader.*

He is also a strong proponent of having reasonable work–life boundaries. He understands that if his leaders and team members are happier at home, they will come to work ready to serve their team and the world community. I was blown away when I heard (in a video) him encouraging his senior leadership to role model work–life integration with this powerful advice:

- Walk into the house with your cell phone, turn it over, and say to your significant other, "Let's connect for the next hour."

- If you receive an email on the weekend, you don't have to respond until Monday unless there is a specific *I need it now* request.

- Let your team know it's okay to go to the gym at lunch.

Alex is a man after my own heart and a great example of a leader who practices intentional attention. As the CEO of a multibillion-dollar company creating products to transform world health, he understands that we can best serve others by being intentional in all aspects of our life.

https://www.jnj.com/_document/our-credo-english?id=00000159-6a64-dba3-afdb-7aef76350000

https://www.youtube.com/watch?v=CJHjXm8koxo

Reduce Stress and Promote Healthy Choices

According to the American Psychological Association, stress plays a major role in the workplace. Consider these statistics:

- More than $500 billion is lost each year from the U.S. economy because of workplace stress.
- 550 million workdays are lost each year due to stress on the job.
- 60 to 80% of workplace accidents are attributed to stress.
- More than 80% of doctor visits are due to stress.
- Workplace stress has been linked to health problems ranging from metabolic syndrome to cardiovascular disease and mortality.

If that isn't enough to make you grab your stress ball and start squeezing, a recent Willis Towers Watson "Staying@Work" survey discovered more fascinating information. In the survey on workplace health and productivity, employees ranked their top stressors and employers ranked what they believe are the top stressors for employees. While employers ranked company culture last on the list of stressors, it was the third choice of employees. "This disconnect underscores the fact that most employers don't understand what causes stress for their employees and often leads them to the wrong solutions," said senior consultant Tom Davenport.

How stressful is your organizational culture?

If you are a C-suite executive, you have the power and influence to craft organizational culture. Even if you're not a high-level executive, you are still the architect of your team's culture. Cultivate an environment that allows them to feel their best and optimize their health with these strategies:

- *Foster unity*—Teams that are united, that get each other and support each other, will always accomplish more with less stress. That sense of unity kicks in when someone is on vacation, sick, caring for an ill child, or has a family emergency. The rest of the team willingly picks up the slack, honors the responsibilities, and keeps the work world spinning, because they understand that if there comes a time when they need a helping hand, someone on the team will do the same for them. That kind of unity starts at the top with leadership. Foster it, model it, and support it throughout your whole team.

- *Encourage power naps*—Follow the example of clever companies like Ben & Jerry's, Zappos, Nike, Google, and Huffington Post, which designate a space to de-stress with such things as Nap Rooms.

- *Start a Gratitude Wall*—Put a huge whiteboard in your offices where team members can encourage one another.

- *Make it fun*—Turn up the fun, and turn down stress levels. Amp up the feeling of community and create the foundation for team cohesiveness. Don't be afraid to get creative.

126

- *Play music*—Some of my clients turn up tunes every morning and everyone does a 15-minute stretch. Or, some call it the Seventh Inning Stretch and power everyone up during the 3 p.m. slump.

- *Use toys*—Some of our clients supply their crew with Nerf guns and randomly ring a bell throughout the week where everyone stops what they're doing for a 15-minute Nerf battle.

- *Host regular company or team events*—Paint ball, bowling, golf tournaments, and broom ball are great group activities. Make time for Fun Fridays where everyone enjoys a fit-friendly potluck lunch.

- *Volunteer together*—Some of our clients, including MTV, Trinity Health, and Johnson & Johnson, volunteer as a group at Habitat for Humanity once a year and spend a day framing houses. Others act as Big Brothers and Big Sisters or form teams and work with the Red Cross and United Way. Ask the team for their suggestions. Volunteering not only benefits worthy organizations but also builds team unity and adds fun to your culture.

- *Exercise together*—Exercise is a great stress reducer and benefits your health. When people exercise together, they develop accountability partnerships that help them stick to goals and make sure no one is going it alone.

  - Start a running group or company basketball, baseball, softball, or soccer team.

  - If there's a gym in your building, help team members have affordable access.

  - Create a *Fitbit step challenge* with weekly step goals. One of our insurance clients, Johnson Kendall Johnson (JKJ), organizes Fitbit step challenges for their clients as well as for their employees. JKJ has won Best Place to Work multiple years in a row.

- *Create a healthier environment*—Encourage team members to take breaks, keep a supply of healthy snacks and fresh water on hand, and add more live plants to the office to purify the air. When working with Paramount Pictures in Hollywood to increase productivity and attention in their new open-plan environment, I was astounded at the incredible focus of leadership to ensure they provided healthy (and delicious) breakfast and snacks to their team. Every fridge was stocked with a variety of foods, and team members were encouraged to meet in the outdoor areas to get fresh air. Their human resource department works closely with leadership to continue to enhance this experience for their team. Viacom (the parent company) is committed to workplace productivity.

- *Reward team members for kicking unhealthy habits*—I've worked with organizations that go the extra mile to ensure their employees' health is a priority. Some offer incentives for employees to stop smoking or consuming sugary drinks. Another idea is to host a fitness contest where the person who loses the most weight in a certain time frame wins a prize or a donation to their charity of choice.

Creating a healthy culture doesn't have to cost a fortune and doesn't require a huge investment of time. It does require a mental shift. "Culture reflects leadership," says John DiJulius, CEO of the DiJulius Group, an organization focused on elevating the customer service experience. John is determined to create a customer service revolution (you can see why we get along so famously). He's right. It starts with you. Culture is often the result of how you take care of your team, not just professionally, but personally. Paying deliberate attention to their physical and mental well-being while they are at work shows your team they are more than just an employee. They are talented, valued, and appreciated team members.

Do you want your organization to be nominated for Best Place to Work? Start by taking care of their health and creating a culture where they don't just survive; they thrive.

STOP THE MEETING MADNESS

Some meetings aren't just a waste of time; they are a waste of money! I guarantee you've sat in many an unproductive meeting that went off topic, had tangential conversations, and didn't cover all the agenda items.

In a study of time budgeting at large corporations, Bain & Company found that a single weekly meeting of midlevel managers was costing one organization $15 million a year!

Read that again—that's insane!

It costs organizations time and money when people gather. It's time to commit to more productive meetings as part of the Attention Revolution.

It is your responsibility as a leader to be engaging and to keep your team's attention during the meeting. If meetings are not effective, it's your fault. That's right. If you don't know how to facilitate a meeting, get training, read books, listen to experts, and watch those you admire. Invest your attention learning this skill and watch your team's productivity sky-rocket.

You can develop a reputation for well-run meetings with these ideas:

- *Read Death by Meeting*—Patrick Lencioni's brilliant book defines four styles of meetings and when to host them.

- *Create an agenda and publish or distribute it ahead of the meeting*—Keep the agenda brief and specific. Use action-oriented words such as *brainstorm, decide, determine next steps, agree on outcomes, finalize the project*, and *debrief.* Distribute the agenda beforehand so that everyone goes into the meeting knowing what will be discussed or what tasks need to be completed, and they will feel more prepared.

- *Stick to the agenda*—Having a solid agenda is just the first step. You actually have to follow it during the meeting. If the meeting veers off course, you have to refocus the group on the task at hand. Use this line to manage disruptive attendees and tangent conversations: "For the sake of time, let's move on."

- *Summarize action steps at the end*—Assign owners and time frames to each action step and ask people to report back between meetings. Meetings with no agreed outcomes are a waste of time.

- *Share goals in every meeting*—Remind team members how every meeting and project aligns to achievement of goals. If it isn't aligned, cancel it.

- *Focus on strategy*—Know the company and team objectives and articulate them regularly.

- *Cancel meetings*—If you don't have the decision maker or the information required to make a decision, cancel the meeting.

- *Shorten meetings*—Take the time you initially plan for a meeting and halve it. Try 30 minutes instead of 60, 15 instead of 30. This forces you to get things done.

- *Consider device-free meetings*—Before the meeting starts, ask everyone to silence and put away their devices.

- *Use video conferencing when you can't meet in person*—I prefer video conferencing to teleconferencing for the ability to look people in the eyes, keep them engaged, and stop multitasking. There are a number of video conference tools that are easy to use, and you can use them to record the meeting.

> Go to neenjames.com/extras for my favorite video-conference services.

- *Schedule walk and talks*—Steve Jobs made a habit of the walking meeting, according to CNNMoney: "Taking a long walk was his preferred way to have a serious conversation." Facebook's Mark Zuckerberg and Jack Dorsey of Twitter are also known to favor walking meetings.

- *Be a role model*—Give the kind of intentional attention in meetings that you want to receive from your meeting attendees:

  - Put your device away!

  - Listen with your eyes. Show you are listening by being involved in the conversation, asking relevant questions, and probing for more answers.

  - Demonstrate engagement through your body language and tone of voice and by actively taking notes.

How much are your meetings costing your organization? If you want to scare yourself, use this meeting cost calculator created by *Harvard Business Review* before your next company meeting at https://hbr.org/2016/01/estimate-the-cost-of-a-meeting-with-this-calculator.

COMMUNICATE CLEARLY WITH CONTEXTUAL MODELS

It should be obvious by now that I think in models. No, not supermodels. Contextual models. Contextual models are extraordinary tools for presenting ideas with more clarity, capturing your unique intellectual property, positioning your message, and providing a framework for others. Famous contextual models include Covey's quadrant model (the urgent versus the important) and the food industry food pyramid.

A great model can take a complex idea and simplify it. Models are amazing tools for capturing attention because their visual nature appeals to so many different learning styles. In any given group, you've got people who are analytical and others who are visual. A contextual model speaks to both the left and right brain hemispheres. It provides the information analytics need to make a decision, and it lays out that information in such a way that it makes sense for those who process information visually. (That whole "seeing is believing" thing is real!)

Listed below is my four-step process for contextual modeling. Clients hire me to create contextual models for their organizational messaging, entrepreneurs hire me to create a model for their unique intellectual property, and I often do live *hot seats* during my keynote speeches. It's always fun to invite an audience member on stage, put them in the hot seat, ask questions, and then, voila, I create a contextual model just for them! Some of my speaker friends have incredible talents like Judson Laipply (famous creator of the first viral video on

YouTube, "Evolution of Dance"); Patrick Henry, a Nashville songwriter who is featured regularly on Sirius radio, and often writes and delivers customized songs for his clients, always making the audience laugh; or Jon Petz, who captivates audiences with real magic tricks all linked to a business message. I can't sing or dance (at least not in public), so this four-step process is my only magic trick!

A powerful contextual model will elevate your message, accelerate your communication, and capture your team's attention and engagement.

- *Step 1: Choose your shape.* When you think of the idea you want to demonstrate in your presentation, training program, or marketing materials, what shape comes to mind? Squares, circles, triangles? If you are sharing a process, maybe that feels like a ladder (a triangle can work well here), or maybe it is about relationships (circles work well or consider a Venn diagram), or maybe you want to compare and contrast ideas (a square as a quadrant model would be a great way to do that or an x/y-axis model).

For a contextual model cheat sheet, go to neenjames .com/extras.

- *Step 2: Choose your main point.* Determine the main point you want the model to convey. Be very clear on one big message or one process; don't complicate your model with mixed messages. Do you want to outline steps in a process, compare information, demonstrate characteristics, or provide outcomes? Once you determine your main message you can then determine how to share them in the model.

- *Step 3: Choose your movement.* Great contextual models also include movement, especially if the message is aspirational. Movement in a model can be shown with an x/y-axis, arrows, or even shading. People should be able to quickly identify where they are on the model and where they may want to go.

- *Step 4: Choose your words.* To ensure your model looks and sounds elegant, pay special attention to the words you use. Are you using formal or casual language? Are you using action-oriented words or descriptive words? I call this your language palette and it needs to be consistent. For example, if you are looking at T-shirts in the store, you can buy small, medium, large, and humungous, right? No! In this sentence, *humungous* is not the word you expected to hear. You thought it was *extra-large* and you're right. Make sure the words you use in the model make sense to the reader.

The next time you need to present a conceptual idea to your team or provide an update of your project to your organization, consider creating a contextual model. You may find the attention it draws will give you just the lift you need to knock it out of the park!

As leaders, we are paid to deliver results. Remember what I said earlier: You and your team don't have time to do everything, only time to do what matters. Clarify priorities and boost productivity and you will see a hefty return on your attention.

Over the last four chapters, we have seen how our attention pays personally and professionally. Personally, we have established the need to create meaning for those we care about, and to be thoughtful with whom we choose to spend our time. Professionally, we have discovered how to proactively eliminate distractions and narrow our focus so we can be more productive. Now, in Chapter 7, we will look at how you can make an impact locally and globally.

Make Your Attention Pay

1. What strategies can you implement at work to minimize stress?

2. How can you empower your team to get more done?

3. What do you need to do to create an agile culture?

4. Can you establish distraction-free zones in your workplace?

PART FOUR

Globally—Be Responsible

CHAPTER 7

Make an Impact: The Great (Disappearing) Barrier Reef

Have you ever wanted to visit one of the seven natural wonders of the world?

Twenty-five years ago, my husband and I stretched our tiny, newlywed budget and treated ourselves to a week in Airlie Beach in Queensland. (If you are looking at a map of Australia, or Oz as we Aussies affectionately call it, that's the pointy part on the right of the map.) We couldn't afford to stay at the fancy resorts on Hamilton Island, so we booked a room at Airlie Beach, a popular and cheap destination for backpackers making their way around Australia.

We enjoyed many day trips to the beautiful islands that form the Great Barrier Reef. One morning we traveled by boat for two hours to the Outer Reef, a less touristy part of the reef. When the boat stopped, we stood on the bow and looked down into the water. The water was alive with vivid colored corals and marine life. When we dove in the water with snorkel and fins, we were surrounded by the brightest colors you can ever imagine. It was like a scene from the movie *Finding Nemo*.

Fast forward to 2016, when my honey and I went back to Queensland. This time we were able to afford to stay at the fancy resort on Hamilton Island. We excitedly took a day trip back to almost the exact spot on the Outer Reef that we had experienced 25 years earlier. With snorkel and fins, we dove back in the water.

Where before there had been magnificent corals, starfish, and anemones, now there were bleached coral, minimal marine life, and so much devastation. My honey and I were so sad; I cried. It was nothing like what we had witnessed all those years ago. If you have never seen it, it is still a thing of beauty, but it was magnified a hundredfold 25 years ago.

This devastation is a result of us not paying attention to our planet.

"The survival of the Great Barrier Reef hinges on urgent moves to cut global warming because nothing else will protect coral from the coming cycle of mass bleaching events," says Terry Hughes. New research from a study authored by 46 scientists of three mass bleaching events on Australian reefs found coral was damaged by underwater heat waves, regardless of any local improvements to water quality or fishing controls.

At this rate of mass bleaching due to global warming, all that will be left of the Great Barrier Reef will be huge white skeletons, devoid of life and color. The researchers went on to say the findings of their research affect coral reefs worldwide.

I want my goddaughters, Maddie and Ava, to experience the Great Barrier Reef one day, and I want there to be something for them to witness. I have a small tattoo on the inside of my right wrist that says, *Be Ah-Mazing*. Yes, that is the spelling on the tattoo. Every day I want to wake up in awe and wonder and say, "Ahhhhhh, that's ah-mazing."

We need to be responsible global citizens and start giving intentional attention to our planet and to our precious resources before they disappear.

YOU CAN MAKE AN IMPACT

In 1987, Ian Kiernan competed in BOC Challenge Solo-Round the World Yacht race. While sailing, he was heartbroken to see the world's oceans filled with huge amounts of rubbish. (That's right. In Australia, we call it rubbish, not trash. That's a little slang lesson for you.)

When he returned to Sydney in 1989, he took action on his mission to inspire the community to get out and clean up the harbor. More than 40,000 people came out to clean the waterways. That was the start of Clean Up Australia Day.

I was at that very first Clean Up Australia Day. I was working at Westpac Banking Corporation. We had heard of Ian's mission, and we put together a team from our local branch to join the effort. I remember it was messy! We were filthy and hot. Yet, we were delighted to be part of something and to be giving our attention to an important cause.

Inspired by the success of that first event, Ian began to wonder what would happen if we mobilized the whole nation. The next year, 300,000 volunteers came out. In the past 26 years, Australians have devoted more than 31 million hours to the environment and collected 331,000 tonnes of rubbish through Clean Up Australia Day.

But Ian didn't stop there. The next step was to take Clean Up Australia Day global. With the support of the United Nations Environment Program, Clean Up the World was launched in 1993. Ian's vision translated into approximately 30 million people in 80 countries in that first year alone coming out to help the planet.

Ian will tell you he's just an average Aussie bloke. He was one man who had a vision, accepted responsibility to make an impact, and took action. His idea inspired others to take action and impact our planet.

Like Ian, it's time for each of us to take full responsibility for how we use our limited resources and the way we treat our planet. Maybe you don't care about the Great Barrier Reef or trash in the waterways. Maybe you are more concerned about the erosion of forests in your area or the lack of clean water in countries around the world. Maybe you'll find a cause as a result of reading this book; I hope so.

Don't undervalue the part we all play. Don't underestimate the cumulative effect and momentum of our collective individual decisions.

As individuals, we can give our attention to how we use resources at home, at work, and when we travel:

- At hotels, reuse your towels, decline unnecessary housekeeping services, and use the recycling options offered.
- Carry a refillable water bottle everywhere.
- Use public transportation or rideshare.
- Avoid grabbing for paper towels so often to clean.
- Stop printing documents unnecessarily.
- Encourage family and team members to actively recycle.
- Use refillable water containers and water services.
- Donate unnecessary furniture and equipment and gently used clothing.

Find something you believe in and think about how you can use your attention, time, and resources to create a bigger impact on that.

LEVERAGE YOUR LEADERSHIP

Several years ago, I was fortunate to be the emcee and closing keynote speaker for the California Nevada Credit Union League. Magic Johnson, the world-famous basketball player, was the opening keynote speaker.

When I first met him—all 6 feet, 9 inches of him—he looked down, smiled, and said, "Neen, you are my twin." He was as delightful on and off the stage as you might imagine. We had so much fun working together—my 4-feet, 10-inch frame beside his, and my little size 5.5 feet wearing his size 14 shoes on stage!

During his presentation, he shared the work he does in his Magic Johnson Foundation and how he wants to create communities where people can flourish. He's the real deal and someone who leverages his celebrity status, wealth, and experience to impact our world.

You may not be a celebrity, but you are a leader and people follow your example. What can you do personally and professionally, with the resources and community you have, to influence others to give intentional attention to our planet?

As a leader of influence, can you:

- Allow team members to take time off to serve in a charity of their choice on a regular basis?
- Include a community-focused activity in your next leadership event?
- Sponsor a section of the city, adopt a highway, or offer support for a protected animal at the zoo that your organization can all get behind?
- Implement an office recycling initiative?
- Replace plastic water bottles with water filling stations and gift each team member a reusable water bottle?

- Encourage clothing drives each year to donate gently used clothing, especially winter coat drives?

- Partner with a food bank and encourage team members to donate regularly?

How can you as a leader encourage your team and organization to get more involved in the community, world events, or worthwhile causes?

ORGANIZATIONAL STEWARDSHIP

There are many ways you and your organization can influence your community and our planet by investing your attention to make an impact.

Create a Connection

Many organizations have found unique ways to make an impact by tying their efforts to their product or service or the way their customers use their product or service. Here are some exciting examples of how companies are implementing programs to help our planet:

- *Mac Makeup* created Back to Mac, a program that allows you to bring back the packaging of any five items and receive a free lipstick in exchange.

- *Brita filters* will send you a free shipping label to return their used filters when you collect five pounds worth. They then recycle them into outdoor furniture, bike racks, and watering cans (Brita.com/recycling filters).

- *Nike* collects over a million pairs of worn-out sneakers every year through its reuse-a-shoe program. They use the recycled shoes to make playgrounds, tracks, and other materials. (Source: *Real Simple* Magazine, October 2017)

- *Marks & Spencer* encourages customers to donate a piece of clothing every time they buy an item at one of its stores. The *shwop bins* (donated clothing collection bins) are eye-catching hot pink bins located in hundreds of Marks & Spencer stores.

- *Starbucks* uses coffee cup sleeves made of recycled paper, saving roughly 78,000 trees per year.

- *Dell* allows customers to return any Dell-branded product back to the company—for free—through its "no computer should go to waste" recycling program.

- *Hewlett Packard* owns and operates enormous e-waste recycling plants that shred discarded, obsolete computer products and turn them into raw materials that can be recycled into the industrial food chain.

- *NYNEX*, a division of Bell Atlantic, recycles old phone books into payment remittance envelopes. The envelopes contain at least 75 percent recycled content.

- *Amazon* started their Give Back Box program to allow users to recycle boxes to ship donations to Goodwill and other charities for no shipping charge.

- *Wyndham Grande in Clearwater, Florida,* provides a recycling bag every day to make it easy for guests and housekeeping to be mindful daily.

Being Responsible Can also Be Profitable

Making an impact is often an altruistic endeavor, but it doesn't have to be. Taking care of our planet and our limited resources is often just good business sense.

EV100, a coalition of global corporations, including Unilever, Ikea, and shipping giant DHL, recently launched a global campaign to accelerate the shift away from gas- and diesel-powered vehicles (which generate 25 percent of energy-related greenhouse gas emissions) to electric vehicles. Since more than half of the cars on the road belong to companies, the shift could have a major impact.

Consider the ways other companies are affecting their bottom line while also making a difference:

- *Bank of America* saved an estimated $483,000 in trash hauling fees by recycling paper.

- Independent tire dealers collect and recycle old rubber tires for a profit.

- Buying in bulk and purchasing office products made from recycled content supports the recycling industry.

- Offering filtered water and replacing disposable plates and cutlery with reusable options saves money.

The Power of Employee Service Days

Many of my clients allow team members to choose one day a year for service to any organization that they believe in. The company pays them for this day.

Comcast Cable is one client whose focus on community service has always impressed me. They created Comcast Cares Day, an idea by the late founder Mr. Ralph Roberts. This day brings together more than 100,000 employees, families, friends, and community partners around the world to volunteer and make an impact in local communities. Since 2001, Comcast Cares Day has contributed more than 5 million total service hours to improve local communities. In 2017, Comcast gave back to over 1,000 projects across 22 countries.

Nova Nordisk may well take the top prize when it comes to providing employees with paid time off to volunteer with an incredible 80 hours (10 days) per year. Community engagement is an integral part of their company culture with programs and resources to help employees give back. In 2014, the company debuted a portal to track and help employees find volunteering opportunities. Most company offsite meetings have a community service component built into them, and there's even a Novo Nordisk Social Awareness Team in charge of organizing community service projects.

Could your organization add a service day to your calendar?

Encouraging and allowing team members to participate in causes they care about improves morale and employee engagement. I invite you to consider how you and your organization can take responsibility and take action to care for our planet for the benefit of everyone now, and in the future.

Have you heard the fable about the hummingbird and the priest?

One day, a kind and gentle priest spoke to a little hummingbird who was hovering outside the church window. "What is the color of the church?" he asked.

The hummingbird looked up and replied, "Why, it is red, of course, my favorite color."

The priest, who stood behind her while she furiously flapped her tiny wings, smiled. The little bird saw only one red panel of a huge, stunning stained-glass window. "Fly a little higher," he encouraged her.

Zipping up and away from her perch, she looked back at the church. She gasped. With her view expanded, she could see the beautiful kaleidoscope of colors before her.

It's easy to have a tiny worldview—to see only what is in front of us. I challenge you to step back and expand your view. Look beyond yourself and your role, and see what is going on in your community and your world.

You have a chance to see our planet for what it is—a magnificent cathedral full of beauty and wonder, filled with people you care about.

How are you giving your attention to our world?

Decide today to make a greater impact with your attention and leave a legacy for those who will follow.

Make Your Attention Pay

1. How can you be more globally focused at home, at work, and in your community?

2. What can you personally do to create a legacy for others?

3. How can your business be more community focused?

CHAPTER 8

Join the Attention Revolution

Congratulations! You invested your attention and made it all the way to the end—go you!

On your journey to be more intentional with your attention, you have learned how to be thoughtful with the people you care about, productive with the actions you take, and responsible for the planet we inhabit. You know how to give attention and to whom, as well as what is important and how to get attention for the people and projects that matter to you. You are now more aware of how intentional attention is conscious rather than unconscious, deliberate rather than distracted, and transformational rather than transactional.

You have discovered how to give intentional attention personally, professionally, and globally. As an individual, you can create more moments of significance. As a leader, you can create a healthy and nurturing environment for you and your team. As a citizen, you can contribute on a greater scale in your wider community. You now have the tools to create meaning, create success, and create a legacy.

It doesn't end here. Your intentional attention journey has just started. You are part of the effort to create an attention-surplus economy.

Let's start the Attention Revolution—together!

There's a reason this is so important to me. You might be surprised to learn I know what it's like to want and yes, even crave attention. I don't want anyone to ever feel invisible. I want every person to feel seen and heard.

I need your help. Let's not stop here. There is never an end; you just keep getting better at it and inspiring others to join you.

Can you share this resource with your team at work?

Can you challenge others to have device-free conversations?

Can you step away from the social media obsession?

Can you cultivate a less stressful, more joyful work environment and encourage collaboration and creativity?

Can you challenge your family when you go home tonight to share a meal together and a real conversation?

You might be sitting there saying, "But, Neen, I just can't do this 100% of the time." You're right. You can't—if you don't try. We are all works in progress, myself included. Do I get it right every day? Nope. Do I want to? Absolutely, yes!

Hanging above my desk is a pottery sign made by world-renowned Bucks County artist Lisa Naples. It has a picture of a bird in the center and the words around the outside are, "Just Be. Notice. Be Present. It's Enough." As soon as I saw it at her studio opening, I wanted to buy it. It has hung on my office wall for over 10 years. It serves as a daily reminder that my attention is valuable and needs to be spent wisely.

Find your own touch point, attention trigger, or reminder. Intentional attention is a daily, deliberate practice. Do we always feel like it? No. Is it always impactful? Yes.

Being an attentive leader requires commitment, focus, and a desire to set free old habits and create new ones. This requires you to make people more important than technology. It also requires you as a leader to go against the norms of what others are doing and implement creative strategies that could truly transform your team and your company.

Are you willing to give up some of those bad habits of constantly being connected?

Are you willing to sit and be alone with your thoughts?

Are you willing to stop emailing team members late at night and stealing minutes from their loved ones?

Are you willing to stop texting and driving? (It might just save your life or the life of someone else.)

Are you willing to reduce your meetings, eliminate unnecessary emails, and stop the busyness that isn't helping you achieve your goals?

Are you willing to invest extra time recycling and be more conscious of this precious planet we are given?

Oliver Wendell Homes said, "One's mind, once stretched by a new idea, never regains its original dimensions."

You now understand the importance of being intentional with your attention. You understand how your focus and your brain can be changed if you are willing to stop these habits. You understand the costs and consequences of not paying attention to people, priorities, and our planet.

I believe in you. I believe that you want to make a difference in the world. I believe you want to be a stronger leader at work and at home. I believe you want to show people they are important to you. So, it's all up to you.

Are you willing to do what it takes to be committed to a new way of paying attention?

An attention revolution begins at home. It means consciously walking into your home and paying deliberate attention to those you love.

It means when you go to work, you stop being busy and start being productive. It means you have to say no to the things that don't matter so you can say yes to things that do.

It means when you travel, in your community, and at your home and workplace, you start to be more responsible for how you use products and services to protect this one planet we have with the limited resources we are given.

When intentional attention is present, you know it.

If you have read this far and you don't apply any of these strategies, that would break my heart. I guess you wouldn't be any worse off than when you started this book. But if you choose today to really focus more intentionally in all aspects of your life, it's not just you that will benefit. It's those around you, it's the company you work with, and the community you are part of.

Don't do it for yourself. Do it for the people you care about. Today, choose one strategy and implement it.

Stop touching your cell phone so many times each day and touch someone you love instead.

Stop answering emails during meetings and instead answer a team member on how they can make a bigger contribution in your organization.

Stop using plastic water bottles and start using a refillable bottle.

Intentional attention is about the choices you make and actions you take.

The choices don't have to be huge; every small action you take makes a greater impact on others.

Constantly ask yourself:

Who needs my attention right now?

What is the best use of my attention right now?

How is the best way to spend my attention right now?
Use that sense of urgency to fuel you.

My goal in writing this book for you and spending time together was to help you *give* the attention others need from you.

My desire for you is that as a result of your investment in others, and your investment in yourself, you will *get* the attention you want for your relationships, your career, and your organization.

We get to design this one life we lead on this one planet. Today, invest one minute, in one interaction, to create one significant moment, for just one person that may create one memory that will last a lifetime.

Bonus Chapter: Build an Organization That Pays Attention

If you want attention to pay in business, you must first *give* attention to *get* attention.

In business conscious, deliberate attention is vital. When you give it to your employees and customers it is nothing short of transformational.

Walt Disney knew that—and he knew it 60 years ago. There's a reason Disney is one of the most heralded benchmarks in business.

If you've ever visited a Disney property, one thing you notice is how clean the parks are. Always. Disney never wanted anyone to walk more than 20 steps to a trashcan, so all the parks are designed that way. What you may not have noticed at Disney is that you never see anyone emptying the trash. Because Walt wanted to ensure your experience was never interrupted by something that could distract from the fun (he was even a forefather of the attention-surplus economy!), he created a revolutionary underground garbage disposal system.

Walt Disney knew intention is an action word. It's about choice. It is the act of paying attention. It is having a purpose, and being deliberate in our actions. Think about all the ways Disney uses intention beyond trash collection. It shows up in their backstage and the way they train cast members—you never see someone out of character. It also shows up in the way they look after every guest. They have cast members who know sign language so they can assist their deaf guests.

Giving intentional attention as a marketing strategy differentiates your organization from your competitors. Competitors are constantly vying for your customer's precious attention in our attention-deficit society. Now more than ever before, companies have realized that to stand out and build loyalty in a cluttered marketplace (where consumers have multiple choices in person and online for every service, at the touch of a button, and can have anything delivered, possibly within a day) requires unique strategies to create significant moments for their customers.

Companies that give intentional attention enjoy:

- Increased sales
- Repeat business
- Loyal customers
- Brand advocacy
- Vendor responsiveness
- Social media reviews
- Community engagement
- Employee top talent
- Awards, including Best Place to Work and Best in the Business

Starbucks founder Howard Schultz once said, "We're in the people business serving coffee, not the coffee business serving people." He knew coffee was a secondary priority; people were first.

Do you and your team always keep in mind that no matter what business you are in, people should be first?

No matter your industry, your product, or your service, or whether customers buy from you online or offline, you are always in the people business first and foremost. That is precisely why giving intentional attention is such a powerful competitive strategy. Remember, it's human nature to want and need attention.

To get and keep your customers' attention and loyalty, you must first give conscious, deliberate, and transformational attention.

Key intentional attention strategies for organizations include empowering team members to give their own intentional attention, bridging the gap between online and in-person experiences, systemizing thoughtfulness, and engaging the senses. Let's look at each of these.

EMPOWER YOUR TEAM TO GIVE INTENTIONAL ATTENTION

During a recent trip to Trader Joe's supermarket, I met Doug. As I placed two Trader Joe's recycled shopping bags on his counter (I'd forgotten my own), I told Doug it was my first visit to Trader Joe's. As soon as he heard me say that, he began ringing a big gold bell at his workstation. His supervisor approached, smiled at me, and Doug shared our conversation, explaining he wanted to give me the recycling bags for free. The supervisor inserted her magic key into the cash register and the fee was voided.

Now, these were not expensive bags. What impressed me was Doug's attentiveness and instant reaction to make sure I was taken care of. The free bags are a simple and clever way to empower team members to delight customers. Of course, I'll be going back to Trader Joe's.

When you proactively empower the team to deliver exceptional service, you will be rewarded with increased sales and long-term client loyalty. Attention pays.

Have you ever traveled through Denver International Airport (DIA)? On one of my many adventures through DIA, I was feeling peckish and entered the restaurant Root Down (I know, it's a weird name). It had been a long day and I was mentally and physically exhausted (clearly, I looked like a mess). And then up walked Linda, my waitperson. She looked me over and said in the most caring way, "Sweetie, you look like you had some kind of day."

She paid extra attention to me at lunch, checked on me several times, refilled my champagne glass, and placed a reassuring hand on my shoulder when I looked up at her in absolute exhaustion with incredible appreciation. You might argue this is part of her job, but she went beyond in terms of giving me attention. I wrote her a quick thank-you note (remember my system for always carrying notecards with me to write a quick note of thanks) and left for my flight.

Fast-forward two months. Back at DIA in Concourse C. Once again feeling peckish, I remembered the great experience at Root Down. It was an easy decision. (Attention pays.) As the maitre d' escorted me to a table, imagine my surprise as Linda came up and gave me a big hug. She said, "I saw you at the front and asked for you to be seated in my section."

How did Linda do that? How did she remember me from all the people she meets each day, all the tens of thousands of people that pass through that airport? She made my whole day! Truth be told, it could have had something to do with the note I left or how I used her name (a *Personally—Be Thoughtful* strategy) on the first visit, something she specifically commented on.

The next day, I keynoted an event for 1,500 meeting professionals at the Denver Convention Center. I shared Linda as a great example of intentional attention. Afterward, several people came up to excitedly tell me, "I know Linda!" or, "I have been served by Linda." She's a true Denver treasure. Linda is a brilliant example of someone who is exceptional at what she does, empowered by leadership to take care of every client, create memories, and develop advocates.

Intentional attention—when given freely—creates a never-ending cycle of expansion that feeds on itself.

Linda gave me intentional attention. I returned it to her and to her restaurant by going back. She returned it to me again, as she had to many other customers as evidenced by the people who came up to me after my speech. I gave attention to her organization in my speech. Of those 1,500 people who were in my audience, how many do you think will go to Root Down the next time they visit DIA? How many of you will visit Root Down when you are at DIA? Attention pays—and it pays directly to the bottom line.

How can you empower your team to surprise and delight your customers with this level of intentional attention?

What training can you provide to demonstrate how to give intentional attention to your clients?

What values do you include when recruiting top talent to take care of your clients?

What incentives do you provide top talent to retain them and build their loyalty so they are proud to work for your brand?

I'm Not a Number

BY PATRICK HENRY

I am not a number, I'm a person.

I am not a number, I'm real.

I have joy and hopes and passion.

I'm not a number, I feel.

I'm not the cancer in room 311, the diabetic in 402.

I'm not a four top in the atrium or the quaint two and a half bath three bedroom.

I'm not the ADHD on the red hall or the lowest test score on the blue.

I'm not a number, I'm a person just like you.

I'm not a half percentage point or a margin call,

The sum of pounds read on a scale.

I'm not row 8 seat 32 or the commission on a sale.

I'm not a case to be managed; I'm not the next in line.

I'm not a double decaf mocha latte or a 20-year term life.

I'm not a number, I'm a person and I demand your respect,

But if you treat me like a number, a number is what you'll get.

You see a number won't stay loyal if there comes a better deal.

A number knows no allegiance because a number cannot feel.

Be kind to me and I'll open my heart.

Invite me in and I'll eagerly take part.

Recognize my significance, celebrate my individuality.

Don't treat me like a number and you'll have my loyalty.

LEVERAGE SOCIAL MEDIA TO SURPRISE AND DELIGHT CUSTOMERS

Social media is a low-cost way to connect deeper with clients, guests, and members. You can leverage social media platforms to surprise and delight buyers by showing you are listening and paying attention. A great example of this is the hotel and hospitality industry actively using social media to connect with guests before, during, and after their stay on property.

The Library Hotel in New York uses modern, online tools to provide old-fashioned personal attention in one of the most competitive cities in the world. With so many hotels and Airbnb options available, they use intentional attention as a competitive advantage.

I surprised one of my dearest friends, Lesley, with a trip to New York to stay at this hotel. Lesley is a professor at Elon University and someone who is also passionate about teaching children to read. This, combined with her deep love of books, made it easy to choose this beautiful property. From the moment we made reservations online until we checked out, this hotel did an exceptional job of paying attention online and in person. Their online registration is easy and allows guests to share information about special occasions or add-ons for their arrival.

Located in midtown, The Library Hotel is in a prime spot, just a 10-minute walk from Times Square and Broadway, and one block from Grand Central Station. With more than 6,000 books in their collection and each of the 10 floors themed after one of the designations of the Dewey Decimal System, it's a book lover's dream. The second-floor library was absolutely one of my favorite spaces in the hotel with constant snacks, great coffee, delicious breakfasts, and afternoon cocktails. Even if your room isn't ready when you check in, they instantly make you feel at home, offering guests an opportunity to freshen up in a special area on the second floor.

After a day of fabulous shopping in SoHo and lunch at my favorite New York restaurant, Balthazar, we checked into our room. We stayed in room 1206, the mythology room with a gorgeous view of the NYC Public Library. The staff had left a birthday card and gift for Lesley. I was super impressed. Then I spied a bottle of my favorite Veuve-Clicquot champagne (they had been visiting my Instagram account) and, wait for it—a note and a book from Balthazar! The note and gift blew me away.

This simple act of watching my social media posts, writing a note, and sharing a book from my favorite local place is the level of attention that has guests returning over and over again! When you choose to proactively engage the team in creating experiences where your customers feel appreciated (online and in person), you develop raving advocates for your brand who often share their enthusiasm for your brand with their communities.

Did I tweet about our experience at the Library Hotel? You bet I did! Did I post on Instagram? Of course! Am I writing about it in my book? Would I highly recommend them to everyone? Absolutely! They are a prime case study in intentional attention.

What can you do in your business to make your clients, customers, members, or patients feel like we did during our Library Hotel experience?

How can you provide exemplary service by checking social media profiles of your clients or visiting their websites?

What policies do you need to update to allow team members to engage in social media conversations with your clients?

SYSTEMIZE THOUGHTFULNESS—THE MENDLOWSKI METHOD

Most people don't enjoy going to the dentist. Me, either—until I met Dr. Mendlowski. He runs a very successful dental practice in Doylestown, Pennsylvania. From the moment you step foot in this small local practice, you feel like you are their most important patient. His receptionist Laurie is a great example of someone who loves what she does and has incredible recall of every patient. When I visit twice a year for cleaning, she remembers what I do, my husband, and our neighbors. What completely grabbed my attention, however, was when I met with Dr. Mendlowski on my second visit. He opened my patient file and it was filled with press clippings from articles where I had been featured.

Dr. Mendlowski demonstrates the power of personal touch in a digital world by creating a system for thoughtfulness for everyone who visits his clinic. He has trained his team to give intentional attention to clients. He saves information that he reads in the local papers and media about all his clients. Dr. Mendlowski wants his patients to feel extra special, especially when they are coming for a service they may not enjoy.

In Chapter 4, we talked about the power of systemized thoughtfulness on a personal level. As a leader, you can also implement a process to systemize thoughtfulness and impact customers across your entire organization. Whether your organization is a Fortune 500 company or a local mom and pop operation, you can systemize intentional attention.

How can you provide systemized thoughtfulness?

What routines could you create to be attentive online and in person to show your clients you see and hear them and they are important to you?

ENSURE CUSTOMERS GET A CONSISTENT EXPERIENCE

In today's business climate, almost every organization interacts with customers both online and in person. The question is, do your customers and clients have the same experience with you no matter how they interact with you?

Customers interact with your organization online through the usual channels such as your website, chat facility, social media platforms, email campaigns, advertisements, apps, and text messages. They also experience your brand through third-party channels that may not even be directly related to your organization such as recommendations on review sites.

Of course, customers interact in person with your team members at your physical locations, through your phone system and in focus groups. Keep in mind that they also experience your brand through the quality of your physical products or your services.

The attention you give customers online and in person must be consistent. Consistency means reliability and dependability in your product or service offering, communication strategies, policies and procedures, training, recruitment, and leadership development (it starts with your people first).

If you want your attention to pay, consider that when people experience your organization and your brand—if it's a positive experience—they want to share it with others. (Social media makes that so easy.) Consistency is vital because when they recommend you to their friends, family, and coworkers, they are trusting that you will deliver the same experience. Their reputation is tied to your reputation.

Inconsistent experiences breed disappointment. In our digital world, people now have multiple and bigger platforms to share their discontent. You don't want to be the recipient of negative attention because you weren't consistent.

Where do you need to revise interactions with your clients online or in person to provide a more consistent experience?

GIVE ATTENTION TO GET ATTENTION

Here are a few more ideas to ensure your intentional attention pays:

- *Mystery shop*—Do you remember what it's like to be a front-line team member in your company? When I worked for Caltex (part of the oil industry in Australia), one of my responsibilities was to design and deliver training programs for franchisee-owned and company-operated stores. Each month, I'd slip into a gas station uniform and pin on a trainee badge to work in the gas stations, testing the training programs I'd developed. This gave me a greater appreciation for the challenges employees faced as well as firsthand knowledge of how employees could better service customers.

  - When was the last time you approached your business as a mystery shopper?

  - When was the last time you called your office or call center?

  - When was the last time you walked in your retail store or office building looking at your facilities through the eyes of your customers, patients, or members?

- *Develop custom events*—One of our clients, Credit Union National Association, hosts targeted niche industry conferences for credit union members. A great event called Experience Learning Live is designed for trainers and learning and development professionals within credit unions. These talented individuals have unique

164

challenges and the conference is specifically geared for them.

- Society for Human Resource Management (SHRM) hosts a fantastic event annually for volunteer leaders of local SHRM chapters to develop leadership skills and assist them in their community roles.

- These examples demonstrate brilliant organizations investing in people, paying intentional attention to specific needs, and then designing learning and networking opportunities to support them.

- What niche events could you host for your team or clients?

- *Create monthly subscriptions*—Sephora cosmetic stores have created strong customer loyalty with their monthly subscription Play Box. Each month, subscribers receive sample-size products with a gift bag, instructions sheet, cards for free in-store demonstrations, and a video showing how to use the products from beauty and style gurus. Genius! By paying attention to their customers' needs, they have created a way to regularly and routinely connect with customers, promote in-store visits, and encourage the purchase of full-size products.

  - What unique action can you take to routinely connect with customers?

- *Leverage existing relationships*—When I was in banking in Australia, we knew it cost $50 to attract a new customer. The bank I worked for realized it was more profitable to pay attention to existing customers by assessing their needs and upselling them. We embarked on an internal campaign to increase the number of products each customer had. We also knew the more products a customer had with us, the more challenging it was for that customer to leave our bank.

165

- What can you offer your existing clients to develop deeper loyalty to your business?

PELOTON: THE POSTER CHILD FOR INTENTIONAL ATTENTION

Peloton is a company that has done a truly remarkable job of using intentional attention as a corporate strategy. And has it ever paid off. They know their riders want lifestyle changes, so they created a technology company that helps people achieve their goals and packaged it in a fun, sexy bike—a bike that goes nowhere! Customers ride spin bikes either in the company's New York studio, or they purchase Peloton brand bikes for use in their homes.

So much about the Peloton brand and their business model helps them grow significantly because they pay attention to their community experience online and offline. John Foley, their CEO, will tell you it's a technology company that has paid attention to every touch point for riders, instructors, and visitors to the New York studio and boutique. Peloton created a culture where instructors and riders have a fun experience together. Every interaction, online, offline, and in person is designed to engage the community. Everything about the Peloton brand (online, on demand, and in person) looks and feels consistent. They pay attention to all the little details.

I'm not only an avid fan of this company; I'm a customer. And it has become my obsession. Not a day goes by when I'm at home that I am not riding my bike, even using the app at the hotel gym when I travel if I can find a spin bike. I even took a trip to Peloton in New York (affectionately called the *mothership*) to ride the bike live in the studio and to meet my favorite instructor, JJ. I'm officially addicted.

Their website is easy to navigate, they offer rides beginning at 4 AM EST, and don't even get me started on the instructors and their insanely fit bodies! My favorite instructor, Jennifer Jacobs (JJ), is smart, dedicated, fit, gorgeous, strong, and the business owner of JMethod Fitness, a spokesperson with abs to die for and a heart as big as her smile. Instructors have their own line of clothing, and the company selects real-life Peloton owners to model outfits for their online store.

Peloton instructors know they will build a bigger and more engaged community by regularly giving shout-outs to riders by name on the live rides (sound familiar?). My rider name is #AussieNeen. They also celebrate milestone rides—that is, 50, 100, and 500 rides. This personal touch keeps riders coming back.

They have done a truly remarkable job of bridging the gap between their online and in-person presence, analyzing every possible touch point for subscribers to enhance the shared experience. They also created clever strategies to bridge the gap for at-home riders who participate in live and on-demand rides, contribute to the Facebook group, and wear the Peloton clothing. They host an annual Home Rider Invasion (HRI) event, encouraging subscribers to travel to New York, visit the studio and boutique, meet the instructors, connect with other riders, and participate in a weekend of activities dedicated to thanking them for their loyalty. Their retail stores around the country also host events encouraging home riders to meet.

Peloton keeps surprising subscribers with new features and workouts (on and off the bike). Regular software updates implement rider suggestions and enhance technology. Maybe that's what it's like for Tesla car owners—they wake up one morning and, voila, their software has been updated. All of a sudden, their car can drive itself!

Here are some other clever ways Peloton pays attention to its subscribers:

- Variety of rides that includes length of ride, style, time-slots, and intensity. Subscribers can take live rides (in real time) and on-demand rides (pre-recorded). They also offer scenic rides, which are not instructor led, but simulate the experience of riding outdoors.

- Diverse instructors who represent multiple communities and travel to retail outlets to meet riders. Instructors also build communities on social media and host private events.

- Extensive list of guided workouts to build strength, practice yoga, and stretch off the bike (called *Beyond the Ride*).

- Handwritten cards and notes from management and instructors to members.

- Subscriber suggestions for rides offered, music playlists, and technology features are regularly incorporated.

- Retail stores allow riders to experience the bike, try on the clothing line, celebrate milestone rides, and meet other riders and instructors at special events.

The community (60,000+ riders strong) on Peloton's private Facebook page has been one of the most interesting insights of my Peloton purchase. They are like a cult, obsessed with rides, health, and even the instructors—in the most positive way. Peloton has created a fun tribe of strangers who hold each other accountable and cheer each other on.

Clearly, their intentional attention has paid and paid very well because they also introduced a new piece of equipment, the Peloton Tread.

BONUS CHAPTER

On November 11, 2017, CEO John Foley posted the following message to the Facebook Peloton group:

Fellow Riders,

There aren't many people in the world who will fully appreciate this graph nor believe my instincts that we will continue to outperform these benchmarks for years to come . . . But I figured that if anyone would believe, it would be you folks . . . the folks who got us here. It is with your support and enthusiasm that I can honestly say that we're going to create one of the most special businesses, brands, and communities of all time . . . in any category. And as we grow, your experience with Peloton will get better and better. That is my commitment to you. Thank you for all that you do to make us . . . one Peloton.

The graph showed they had grown faster than Facebook, Apple, and Google in the past four years. At the time of writing, they were valued at over $1.25 billion and growing fast.

What do you need to do to make your customer experience more engaging and make your clients feel like they matter to your organization?

How can you create an experience for your buyers that makes them want to return to you time and time again and recommend you to others?

Intentional attention is a marketing strategy. Intentional attention is a profit strategy. To drive bottom line results for your organization, take notice, make changes, listen more intently, and develop systems that will make your attention pay, every time.

> For a complete list of tools and additional resources for you and your team, go to https://neenjames.com/extras.

Endnotes

INTRODUCTION: DOES YOUR ATTENTION PAY?

Neen James, "Keynote Speaker & Leadership Coach," accessed November 12, 2017. https://neenjames.com.

CHAPTER 1: OUR ATTENTION-DEFICIT SOCIETY

Chris Anderson, *Free: How Today's Smartest Businesses Profit by Giving Something for Nothing* (London: RH Business Books, 2010).

Saga Briggs, "6 Ways Digital Media Impacts the Brain," InformED, September 12, 2016, accessed November 12, 2017, https://www.opencolleges.edu.au/infor med/features/5-ways-digital-media-impacts-brain/.

Lance Brown, "New Harvard Study Shows Why Social Media Is So Addictive for Many," WTWH Marketing Lab, May 11, 2012, accessed November 12, 2017, http://marketing.wtwhmedia.com/new-harvard-study-shows-why-social-media-is-so-addictive-for-many.

Chris Clugston, "Increasing Global Nonrenewable Natural Resource Scarcity— An Analysis," *Resilience*, April 6, 2010, accessed November 12, 2017, http://www.resilience.org/stories/2010-04-06/increasing-global-nonrenewable-natural-resource-scarcity%E2%80%94-analysis/.

Mike Elgan, "Social Media Addiction Is a Bigger Problem than You Think," *Computerworld*, December 14, 2015, accessed November 12, 2017, https://www.computerworld.com/article/3014439/internet/social-media-addiction-is-a-bigger-problem-than-you-think.html?page=5.

ENDNOTES

Megan Erickson, "Will the Next War Be Fought Over Water?" *Big Think*, December 23, 2011, accessed November 12, 2017, http://bigthink.com/re-envision-toyota-blog/will-the-next-war-be-fought-over-water.

Susanna Huth, "Employees Waste 759 Hours Each Year Due to Workplace Distractions," *The Telegraph*, June 22, 2015, accessed November 12, 2017, http://www.telegraph.co.uk/finance/jobs/11691728/Employees-waste-759-hours-each-year-due-to-workplace-distractions.html.

Neen James, "Keynote Speaker & Leadership Coach," accessed November 12, 2017, https://neenjames.com.

Nicholas Kardaras, *Glow Kids: How Screen Addiction Is Hijacking Our Kids—and How to Break the Trance* (New York: St. Martin's Griffin, 2017).

Razali Salleh Mohd, "Life Event, Stress and Illness," *The Malaysian Journal of Medical Sciences* 15, no. 4 (October 2008): 9–18, accessed November 12, 2017, https://www.ncbi.nlm.nih.gov/pmc/articles/PMC3341916/.

Adrian C. Ott, *The 24-Hour Customer: New Rules for Winning in a Time-Starved, Always-Connected Economy* (New York: HarperBusiness, 2010).

Ott, Adrian. "Infographic: Is Information Overload Over-Hyped?" *Fast Company*, September 30, 2012. Accessed November 12, 2017. https://www.fastcompany.com/1688458/infographic-information-overload-over-hyped.

Ted Ranosa, "Humans: Cause of Extinction of Nearly 500 Species Since 1900," *Tech Times*, June 30, 2015, accessed November 12, 2017, http://www.techtimes.com/articles/64542/20150630/humans-cause-of-extinction-of-nearly-500-species-since-1900.htm.

Eric Ries and Ursula Bischoff, Lean Startup: Schnell, risikolos und erfolgreich Unternehmen Grüden. München, Germany: Redline-Verlag, 2012.

Scott Stratten and Alison Kramer, *UnMarketing: Everything Has Changed and Nothing Is Different* (Hoboken, NJ: Wiley, 2017).

"U.S. Businesses Lose Approximately $11 Billion Annually Due to Employee Turnover," Strategy Meets Performance, accessed November 12, 2017, http://strategymeetsperformance.com/facts/u-s-businesses-lose-approximately-11-billion-annually-due-to-employee-turnover/.

Simon Worrall, "How the Current Mass Extinction of Animals Threatens Humans," *National Geographic, August 20*, 2014, https://news.nationalgeographic.com/news/2014/08/140820-extinction-crows-penguins-dinosaurs-asteroid-sydney-booktalk.

"2015 Stress in America," American Psychological Association, accessed November 12, 2017, http://www.apa.org/news/press/releases/stress/2015/snapshot.aspx.

The National Academy of Sciences of the USA, 2009, http://www.pnas.org/content/106/3/912.full.pdf

The World Unplugged, a global study of university students' media habits was led by the International Center for Media & the Public Agenda (ICMPA) in partnership with the Salzburg Academy on Media & Global Change. https://icmpa.umd.edu/portfolio/the-world-unplugged/

Consumer Snapshots – Netflix Streamers, July 1, 2015, exstreamist.com

Dscout, June 15, 2016, http://blog.dscout.com/hubfs/downloads/dscout_mobile_touches_study_2016.pdf?hsCtaTracking=9b6ffb9f-3c60-489f-8599-e6a8d954b7df%7C6f4e83c4-70ee-4bbb-8e81-cd47f5f376fa .

GfK Public Affairs & Corporate Communications, July 2014, https://www.projecttimeoff.com/sites/default/files/PTO_OverwhelmedAmerica_Report.pdf

CHAPTER 2: LISTEN WITH YOUR EYES: THE POWER OF INTENTIONAL ATTENTION

Phillippa Lally, Phillippa, Cornelia H. M. van Jaarsveld, Henry W. W. Potts, and Jane Wardle, "How Are Habits Formed: Modelling Habit Formation in the Real World," *European Journal of Social Psychology* 40, no. 6 (October 2010): 998–1009, accessed November 12, 2017, http://onlinelibrary.wiley.com/doi/10.1002/ejsp.674/abstract.

Saul McLeod, Saul. "Selective Attention," *Simply Psychology*, 2008, accessed November 12, 2017, https://www.simplypsychology.org/attention-models.html.

CHAPTER 3: PERSONALIZE PERFORMANCE: BRAND BUILDING, NIDO QUBEIN STYLE

Chad Hymas, *Doing What Must Be Done: Even Limitations Can Be Used to Make Life Better* (Rush Valley, UT: Chad Hymas, 2012).

Neen James, "Keynote Speaker & Leadership Coach," accessed November 12, 2017, https://neenjames.com/.

Neen James, *Folding Time: How to Achieve Twice as Much in Half the Time* (Doylestown, PA: Neen James Communications, 2013).

Parker J. Palmer, *Let Your Life Speak: Listening for the Voice of Vocation.* (Hoboken, NJ: Wiley, 2009).

CHAPTER 4: FOCUS ON VIPS: SYSTEMATIZE THOUGHTFULNESS

Mike Myatt, "10 Reasons Your Top Talent Will Leave You," *Forbes*, December 13, 2012, accessed November 12, 2017, https://www.forbes.com/sites/mikemyatt/2012/12/13/10-reasons-your-top-talent-will-leave-you/#3c8c812338a6.

Brenda Ueland and Cynthia Miller, *Tell Me More: On the Fine Art of Listening* (Tucson, AZ: Kore Press, 1998).

"2012 Global Workforce Study," Willis Towers Watson, July 2012, accessed November 12, 2017, https://www.towerswatson.com/Insights/IC-Types/Survey-Research-Results/2012/07/2012 Towers-Watson-Global-Workforce-Study.

http://www.octanner.com/content/dam/oc-tanner/documents/global-research/2012-Towers-Watson-Global-Workforce-Study.pdf

CHAPTER 5: PRIORITIZE YOUR PRIORITIES: CREATE SIGNIFICANT MOMENTS

Michael Chui, James Manyika, Jacques Bughin, Richard Dobbs, Charles Roxburgh, Hugo Sarrazin, Geoffrey Sands, and Magdalena Westergren, "The Social Economy: Unlocking Value and Productivity through Social Technologies," McKinsey Global Institute, July 2012, accessed November 13, 2017, https://www.mckinsey.com/industries/high-tech/our-insights/the-social-economy.

David Coleiro, "Do You Truly Understand How Human Decision Making Is Impacting Your Brand?" *Strategic North*, July 12, 2017, http://www.strategicnorth.com/blog/2016/07/12/how-do-humans-make-decisions-and-how-do-those-decisions-lead-to-actions/.

Kostadin Kushlev and Elizabeth W. Dunn, "Checking Email Less Frequently Reduces Stress," *Computers in Human Behavior* 43 (February 2015): 220–228, http://www.sciencedirect.com/science/article/pii/S0747563214005810.

Thoroug book of Quotations, https://books.google.com/books?id=yglLCAgAAQ BAJ&printsec=frontcover&dq=Our+life+is+frittered+away+by+detail. +Simplify.+Simplify.%E2%80%9D&hl=en&sa=X&ved=0ahUKEwiG09fHm ZvYAhVGPN8KHXiDAN4Q6AEIRTAF#v=onepage&q=Our%20life%20is %20frittered%20away%20by%20detail.%20Simplify.%20Simplify.%E2%80% 9D&f=false.

John Haltiwanger, "The Science Of Simplicity: Why Successful People Wear The Same Thing Every Day," November 14, 2014. https://www. elitedaily.com/money/science-simplicity-successful-people-wear-thing-every-day/849141

CHAPTER 6: CREATE A CULTURE OF ATTENTION: STOP THE MADNESS

"Estimate the Cost of a Meeting with This Calculator," *Harvard Business Review*, January 11, 2016, accessed November 13, 2017, https://hbr.org/2016/01/ estimate-the-cost-of-a-meeting-with-this-calculator.

Jessica Gross, "Walking Meetings? 5 Surprising Thinkers Who Swore by Them," TED Blog, April 29, 2013, accessed November 13, 2017, http://blog.ted .com/walking-meetings-5-surprising-thinkers-who-swore-by-them/.

Vanessa Ko, "Let's Take a Walk: A Push for Meetings on the Move," CNN, March 21, 2013, accessed November 13, 2017, http://edition.cnn.com/2013/03/20/ business/walking-meetings/index.html.

Patrick Lencioni, *Death by Meeting: A Leadership Fable—about Solving the Most Painful Problem in Business* (San Francisco, CA: Jossey-Bass, 2004).

"New Research Reveals Biggest Productivity Killers for America's Workforce," Cornerstone OnDemand, November 10, 2014, accessed November 13, 2017, https://www.cornerstoneondemand.com/company/news/press-releases/ new-research-reveals-biggest-productivity-killers-america%E2%80%99s-workforce.

Rita Pyrillis, "Employers Missing the Point of Rising Employee Stress," *Workforce*, March 14, 2017, accessed November 13, 2017, https://www.workforce.com/ 2017/03/14/employers-missing-point-rising-employee-stress.

Emma Seppala and Kim Cameron, "Proof That Positive Work Cultures Are More Productive," *Harvard Business Review*, December 1, 2015, accessed November 13, 2017, https://hbr.org/2015/12/proof-that-positive-work-cultures-are-more-productive.

"What Percentage of Your Life Will You Spend at Work?" ReviseSociology, August 16, 2016, accessed November 13, 2017, https://revisesociology.com/2016/08/16/percentage-life-work/.

"Sleeping at Work: Companies with Nap Rooms and Snooze-Friendly Policies," https://sleep.org/articles/sleeping-work-companies-nap-rooms-snooze-friendly-policies/

CHAPTER 7: MAKE AN IMPACT: THE GREAT (DISAPPEARING) BARRIER REEF

Peter Fairley, "10 Giant Companies Commit to Electric Vehicles, Sending Auto Industry a Message," InsideClimate News, September 19, 2017, accessed November 13, 2017, https://insideclimatenews.org/news/19092017/electric-cars-ev100-coalition-charging-fleet-ikea dhl.

Joshua Robertson, "Only an End to Global Warming Can Save the Great Barrier Reef," *Wired*, March 21, 2017, accessed November 13, 2017. https://www.wired.com/2017/03/end-global-warming-can-save-great-barrier-reef/.

BONUS CHAPTER: BUILD AN ORGANIZATION THAT PAYS ATTENTION

Emily Cohn, "A Billion-Dollar Fitness Startup That Came out of Nowhere Could Kill SoulCycle." *Business Insider*, May 25, 2017, accessed November 14, 2017, http://www.businessinsider.com/peloton-is-now-worth-more-than-1-billion-2017-5.

John Foley, Facebook—Official Peloton Group, accessed November 14, 2017, https://www.facebook.com/photo.php?fbid=10104183947846771&set=gm.1759083194395496&type=3&theater&ifg=1.

Index

Index

INDEX